ISLAM AT A GLANCE

ISLAM AT A GLANCE

by
Sadruddin Islahi

Translated by
M. Zafar Iqbal

Islamic Book Trust
Kuala Lumpur

© Human Welfare Trust (Regd.), Delhi
ISBN 983-9154-32-X

First published 1998 by
Markazi Maktaba Islami Publishers, Delhi

This edition by
Islamic Book Trust
607 Mutiara Majestic
Jalan Othman
46000 Petaling Jaya
Malaysia
Email: ibtkl@pd.jaring.my
Website: www.ibtbooks.com

Printed in Malaysia.

CONTENTS

PREFACE

A book which comprised the essential introduction to Islam has long been urgently needed. The ideal thing would be a book neither too academic in approach nor much concerned with details, a compilation in fact neither over-emphasising any aspect nor understating some others but presenting a clear, simple and lucid exposition of Islam, a book plainly stating the genius of Islam, revealing its essence, spelling out its ideals, expounding its cardinal principles and teachings and bringing the whole Islamic order in focus, disclosing the way of life Islam prescribes and the code it enjoins its believers to follow. The present volume is the result of an urge for such a book. I have earnestly endeavoured that it should meet the requirements I have mentioned above. I have tried that those who, in spite of being Muslims, do not have a correct knowledge of Islam, should be able, by going through its pages, to see Islam in its true shape. While the measure of success I have achieved in my effort is purely because of the benevolence of Allah, the failure in the fulfilment of this objective is entirely due to my lack of knowledge and intellect in doing full justice to the subject.

In this book the readers will find both precision and detail. I have employed these devices according the requircment of each subject. I thought it apt to avoid lengthy debate on those religious topics which are either very well known or are usually stressed upon by those who write and speak about Islam or preach it. Those religious matters and aspects which do not fall into this category, on which people are usually inadequately informed and to which the writers and orators also pay scant attention, required comprehensive treatment. Similarly all such religious aspects of which people have not only scant knowledge but are even misinformed about and the full importance of which is not adequately recognized, undeniably deserved to be discussed and argued in detail.

I pray to Allah, and request the readers to endòrse this prayer wholeheartedly, that may this book fulfil the objective it has been written with. May it prove for the people a source of understanding Islam, and for me, its sinful author, something which might be of some help to me in the Afterlife. Amin!

SADRUDDIN ISLAHI

1

CONCEPT AND MEANING

Basic Concepts of Islam

In Arabic "Islam" literally means submission but when the term is used in a religious context it means submission to Allah alone. Accordingly, a Muslim is one who submits to the Divine injunctions and does not deviate from them.

Inherent Islam

We all know that there are two types of Divine injunctions: one is inherent and the other is voluntary.

Inherent injunctions are those which are unavoidable. It is impossible for anyone to defy them. All creatures are so made that they are bound to submit to these injunctions and they are by birth deprived of any discretion of choosing between submission or defiance of inherent injunctions. For instance, the sun has been ordered to rise and act at an appointed time. It has to stay away at a fixed distance from the earth and provide light and warmth to it. The sun has to follow these injunctions and it is not in its power to defy them. Similar is the case of the air which sustains things which are alive. Likewise, water is ordered to slake thirst, fire is ordered to burn, man is ordered to speak with his tongue, hear with his ears and smell with his nose and all of them are bound to obey these injunctions meticulously. These are inherent injunctions and are usually known as physical laws or laws of nature.

All such injunctions of Allah which we are not bound to obey because of any inherent compulsion are optional injunctions. We have a choice to obey or disobey these injunctions. For instance, man is enjoined to worship one God but he is not bound to do so because this injunction is not irresistible in its nature. Instead, he has been given the discretion to worship either one God or add a thousand others with Him or be an atheist altogether. Such injunctions are also called injunctions of Shari'ah or the laws of Shari'ah.

Both these types of injunctions are Divine in equal degree. Since the submission to Allah is Islam, adherence to each of these laws will amount to Islam. It is something quite obvious.

As there is nothing in the universe, right from lifeless objects to men and angels, which does not submit to its Creator or is not subject to the inherent or optional injunctions, the question of Islam or being a Muslim is not restricted to man alone but covers the entire universe. Thus Islam does not remain the religion of any special category of creatures and becomes the religion of all without any exception. It means that Islam is the religion of such things also which have been denied the qualities of will and discretion and are subject to physical laws. As these objects meticulously adhere to the laws enjoined upon them, they are not only Muslims, but perfectly so. The Sun is a Muslim as it faithfully follows the rules it has been subjected to. It revolves, generates heat and light, rises and sets under a regular system. The Moon and the stars are Muslims because they never violate the laws framed for them. The air is Muslim because it blows, tends the clouds, nourishes the plants and provides life to the living beings in the manner prescribed for it. The water is Muslim as it provides fertility to the land, helps plants to grow, satiates thirst and evaporates when heated as this is the duty assigned to it by its Creator.

The fact that the religion of all such objects which do not possess the qualities of will and discretion is Islam, and they are all Muslims, is not based on mere reason or presumption but is founded on these explicit verses of the Holy Qur'an. It says,

Seek they other than the religion of Allah when unto Him submitteth whosoever is in the heavens and the earth, willingly or unwillingly. (3: 3).

These words prove that all things be they in the heavens or on earth, except those men and the jinns who defy the true religion, submit to Allah and their religion is Islam.

Here is another verse of the Qur'an which refers to the same fact in different words:

The seven heavens and the earth and all that therein praise Him, and there is not a thing but hymneth His praise; but ye understand not their praise (17: 44).

In another verses of the Qur'an it is said:

Hast thou not seen that unto Allah payeth adoration whosoever is in the heavens and whosoever is in the earth, and the sun, and the moon and the stars, and the hills, and the trees, and the beasts and many of mankind (22: 18).

These verses make it obvious that it is not one or two particular categories of creatures who praise and glorify Allah but everything, the sky, the earth, the moon, the sun, the stars, the planets, the air and the water, the trees and the plants, the birds and the beasts, men and the jinns, in short every creature from atom to the sun, big or small, animate or inanimate, wise or unwise praises Allah and submits to Him. The least possible meaning of this submission is that all these things adhere to and comply with the Divine injunctions enjoined upon them and bear witness to His being and attributes.

These verses make it abundantly clear that the religion of all such creatures who are devoid of the faculties of will and power is also Islam. But since the injunctions enjoined upon them are of the nature of physical laws their Islam is inherent or inborn rather than optional in character. As such they will be called born Muslims.

Voluntary or Terminological Islam

Let us consider the case of creatures who are endowed with freedom of will and choice. They are so constituted that in certain matters they are helpless, like the former category of creatures, while in others' they are not. In such cases, they enjoy a birth-right of following a course of their own choice. For instance, there are the Divine injunctions enjoining man to see with his eyes, hear with his ears, speak with his tongue. Then there are other Divine injunctions enjoining him to see, hear and say certain things and refrain from others. Man is bound to comply with the former as he has no choice but to obey them. He is compelled to act in accordance with the Divine injunctions. But in the case of the latter, he has no such compulsion. Obedience of these injunctions is a matter of his own choice and liking. He is free to obey or deviate from them. Since within the framework of physical laws, the submission of every individual is characterised as inherent Islam, in other spheres, where man is free to exercise his discretion, his submission to the Divine injunctions will be regarded voluntary Islam. But in the context of religion this term is used without the qualifying words "inherent" or "voluntary". Instead, the terms used for this purpose are "Divine injunctions" and "Islam." The reason for the adoption of these terms is obvious. For such creatures as are subject to both the types of Divine injunctions, physical laws remain of little importance for submission and what really matter are the voluntary injunctions. This is why in day to day conversation the terms "Divine injunctions" and "Islam" are used in place of voluntary injunctions.

This fact also necessitated that the term "Muslim" should not be used for those who do not submit to the Divine injunctions. Although, even in that position, they will still be submitting to the physical laws, and to that extent they will be Muslims. As in the absence of voluntary Islam, inherent Islam becomes meaningless, and it carries no weight. In terms of religion a person is called Muslim only when he proceeds farther than the inherent injunctions and submits himself voluntarily to the optional injunctions.

Islam and Man

As mentioned earlier man is also one of such creatures as are endowed with the faculty of will and choice. He is not only one of them but even distinguished among them. That is why he has also been given Divine injunctions (*Tashri'i* injunctions). The Holy Qur'an says that when the first man was sent to live on this earth, Allah decreed:

> *But verily there cometh unto you from Me a guidance and whoso follows My guidance, there shall no fear come upon them neither shall they grieve. But they who disbelieve, and deny our revelations, such are rightful owners of the Fire* (2: 38-39).

In this decree the sending of the Guidance, that is, Divine injunctions, is conditioned with the word "If". In fact it is not a condition but majesticity of style and what it really means here is that My injunctions will come to you and you shall have to follow them.

What really happened is elucidated in the following verse of the Holy Qur'an:

> *And there is not a nation but a warner hath passed among them* (35: 24)

Both these verses explicitly state that the life of man on this earth and the coming of the Divine injunctions began simultaneously and this world has never been without a religion and a Divine law (Shari'ah) and there has not been a nation who was kept uninformed and deprived of the Divine guidance. Man, being a creature of will and choice necessitated it.

The Religion of Every Nation was Islam

As all the codes of Divine injunctions which have come to Man from the day of the creation to this day, were sent by Allah, submission to each of them was submission to Allah. Therefore, each of these religions was nothing but Islam, and their followers were in fact Muslims. It is a conclusion on which the verdict of reason, and the evidence of the Holy Qur'an are in full agreement. About the Prophet Abraham (a.s.[1]) the Qur'an says:

Abraham was not a Jew, nor yet a Christian, but he was an upright man who had surrendered (to Allah) (3: 67).

Elsewhere it says about Abraham and His Children Isma'il, Ishaq, Ya'qub, Yusuf (a.s.).

When his Lord said unto him: Surrender! he said, I have surrendered to the Lord of the worlds. The same did Abraham enjoin upon his sons and also Ya'qub, (saying): O my sons! Lo! Allah hath chosen for you the (true) religion therefore die not save as men who have surrendered (unto Him.)... .... They said: we shall worship thy God... ... and unto Him we have surrendered (2: 131-133).

Such elucidations have also been made in the Qur'an about Lot (Lut), Moses (Musa), Solomon (Sulaiman), Jesus (Isa) and other Prophets (a.s.) and it is explicitly stated that they and their followers, all of them, were Muslims, and their religion was Islam.

Islam Is the Name of the Ultimate Religion Only

In view of the fact mentioned above; apparently, there should not be any kind of discrimination concerning name and interpretation among the Divine religions. Every Divine religion whether it is guided (Shari'ah) by the Qur'an or by the Torah, the religion of Adam or Noah, the guidance bestowed on Abraham or Jesus—the name of every religion should be Islam and its followers should be Muslims

---

[1] *'alaihi ssalam* (peace be upon him) or *'alaihimu ssalam* (peace be upon them) as the case may be: invocations on hearing the names of prophets who appeared before the Prophet Muhammad *s.a.w.*

because by virtue of their origin and reality all these Divine Codes (Shari'ah) were Islam and their followers were Muslims. But the actual position is otherwise. It is quite the contrary. In the special terminology of the Qur'an, Islam is the name of that religion which it presents itself and which was revealed to the last of the Prophets Muhammad *s.a.w*[2]. Similarly the name of title "Muslim" is also reserved for the followers of this last religion. Thus, when the Qur'an uses the word Al-Islam, it does not do it in its ordinary sense but refers specifically to this one religion and its code of injunctions. For example:

> *This day have I perfected your religion for you and completed My favour unto you, and have chosen for you as religion Al-Islam* (5:3).

> *Lo! Religion with Allah (is) Islam (the Surrender to His will and guidance* (3:19).

In these verses the word Al-Islam explicitly denotes the one religion which was revealed by the Qur'an and the Prophet Muhammad *s.a.w.*

As far as the name "Muslim" is concerned its case is even more clear. The Qur'an says:

> *He hath named you Muslims of old time and in this (Scripture)* (22: 78).

These words are quite clear in their meanings. They say in very decisive tone that all such people who accepted the faith of any prophet were Muslims. However, this honour is reserved only for the believers of the ultimate religion that besides being a Muslim in spirit, they also bear the name of Muslims. Excepting the believers of the last of the Prophets Muhammad *s.a.w.*, no other community of

---

[2] Abbreviation for *Sallallahu 'alaihi wassalm* meaning 'Peace and blessings of Allah be upon him'. This salutation is invoked by the believers each time the Prophet's name is mentioned.

believers was named Muslim. If any community had ever been named Muslim, the saying "He hath named you Muslim", would be altogether unnecessary. Because if all the believers were Muslims by name, there was no need to specify any particular community as Muslim. Thus, whenever the Qur'an calls any other community of believers as Muslims (as it does quite frequently) what is meant is the spirit behind the word. We better say, Islam was their attribute and not their name or title.

Reason for Distinction

It can be asked why this distinction has been made after all? When the religions brought by the other Prophets were sent by Allah in the same way as the one brought by the Holy Prophet Muhammad *s.a.w.* and their followers were as much obedient to Allah as the followers of this ultimate religion, why the name of this religion alone is Islam and why are only its followers called Muslims? If actually all the religions were similar to Islam, and the followers of all other religions were Muslim, why were all them not named Islam and Muslim respectively? It was not done without reason. This allotment of name conforms to the universally accepted and vital principle in vogue for denomination which enjoins that if a particular quality is found in many persons, then he alone deserves to be called after the name and title of that quality who possesses it in the highest degree. If a quality becomes the name of someone, it is a proof of the fact that in him that quality has attained a level of perfection, although it may also be found in others in a lesser degree. In this respect he would be like the Sun before whom the stars pale in significance. For example truthfulness is a quality bestowed upon a multitude of men but the word "Truthful" is a title reserved for Abu Bakr (*r.a.*[3]). It does not mean at all that it was he alone who attained the state of "truthfulness" and all other companions of the Holy Prophet *s.a.w.*

---

[3] *Radiallahu 'anhu, 'anha, 'anhuma or 'anhum* (May Allah be pleased with him, her, the two of them, or them, as the case may be). Salutations reserved for the companions of the Prophet s.a.w.

lacked this quality. Indeed there were some among them about whom the Holy Prophet *s.a.w.* said that if the Prophethood had not come to a close, they would have been Prophets. In short, it can be said with confidence that in this pious group of his companions, there were not one or two but innumerable truthful persons. This being the position, the unique honour of the title of the "Truthful" was conferred upon Abu Bakr *(r.a.)*, evidently for the sole reason that in degree of truthfulness he excelled all others. The pages of history, biographies of the Holy Prophet *s.a.w.* and the traditions bear abundant witness to this effect. The case of the religion revealed by the Holy Prophet Muhammad *s.a.w.* and other Prophets *(a.s.)* may be considered on the above-mentioned criterion. It will be agreed that even though in spirit all religions were similar to Islam, the religion which came in the form of the Qur'an and was brought by the last of the prophets alone deserves the title of Islam because in Islamic attribute it excels all other religions. In comparison to others, it decidedly occupies a much elevated position. Every religion, other than Islam, was such that its code of injunctions was brief and limited, was addressed to a small group of people and the duration of its enforcement was also short. But the case of Islam is quite different. Its code of injunctions is comprehensive and universal, is addressed to the entire humanity and the period of its enforcement is unending. It is meant for the whole world. Its inherent character is consonant with the natural conditions and instincts of humanity. Its teachings constitute an accomplished and perfect way of life. In this religion is perfected the Divine gift and guidance which began from the times of Adam *a.s.* It was, therefore, eminently fair that Islam should have been the name of the last and the most universal and highly accomplished religion.

For similar reasons, the followers of the Prophet Muhammad *s.a.w.* were given the name and title of "Muslims". In their Muslim character they were far more accomplished than the others. They were the flag-bearers of a religion which had no parallel in comprehensiveness, vastness and nobility of objectives. They were assigned the responsibility of carrying on, till the Day of Resurrection, the message of Allah to each and every nation. They were commissioned to bear witness to Islam throughout the world. They are enjoined not to take a moments rest until this righteous religion is spread in every nook and corner of the world.

No other nation was ever assigned such a heavy responsibility. This is why they are called "the best of the peoples" and the name of "Muslims" is also reserved for them.

These details make it clear that although inherently the whole universe is Muslim and all such peoples who followed a Divine religion were Muslims and every religion sent by Allah was Islam, still when the words Islam and Muslim are used, "Islam" denotes the religion brought by the Prophet Muhammad *s.a.w.* and "Muslim" stands for him who professes this religion and follows it.

2

FUNDAMENTAL BELIEFS

In principle as well as in practice the teachings of Islam vary in degree of importance. There exists a natural sequence in them. Some of the teachings are like the foundations. Others are like walls and pillars. Some of them are like roofs and others are like decorative material. For a correct understanding of Islam it is necessary that the study of its teachings is made in this very sequence. We, therefore, take up first of all such teachings of Islam which are of basic importance. In religious terminology they are called "beliefs".

One does not need any agreement to regard beliefs as the basis of religion. While beliefs are the principles, all the rest of the religion is practice. The former has in any case precedence over the latter. The practices is like a tree of which the beliefs are the seeds. As the existence of a tree without its seeds is not possible, likewise practice without beliefs is not possible. Therefore, unless the beliefs exist, the rest of Islam cannot be formulated. The Qur'an says:

But righteous is he who believeth in Allah and the Last Day and the Angels and the Scriptures and the Prophets (2: 177).

It leads us to the conclusion that in the absence of beliefs, piety and good deeds cannot possibly exist. These beliefs (or the articles of faith) of Islam are five in number and has been mentioned in *Ayat-i-Karimah* and other verses of the Qur'an. These articles of faith enjoin:

(1)   Belief in Allah;

(2)   Belief in the Day of Judgement;

(3) Belief in the Prophets;

(4) Belief in the Scriptures; and

(5) Belief in the Angels.

But the traditions of the Holy Prophet *s.a.w.* reveal that in addition to the above five beliefs there is one more article of faith and it is fate. For instance it occurs in the tradition that once Gabriel asked the Holy Prophet *s.a.w.* "What is faith ?" He replied:

"You affirm your faith in Allah, His Angels, His Books, His Messengers, in the Hereafter and you affirm your faith in the Divine Decree to good and evil" (*Muslim*: Faith).

But it does not mean that in this context the Qur'an and the tradition are at variance. It is only a difference of precision and detail. In fact belief in fate is a part of the belief in Allah. This is why the Qur'an has not mentioned it separately. In view of certain exigencies it has been separately mentioned by name in the traditions. As such, belief in fate is as important as belief in the other attributes of Allah and their implications.

The above mentioned six articles of faith have given shape to the entire Islamic system.

But the study of these articles of faith reveals that in degree of importance they are not equal. Some of them are more important, than the others. If they are broadly divided the first three of them will be found of basic importance. The remaining three articles are actually their off-shoots or logical conclusions. If the first three articles of faith are fully understood they will make the whole proposition clear.

3

BELIEF IN ALLAH

Meaning of Belief in Allah

Belief in Allah means:

1. Belief in His existence;

2. Attestation of all His Divine attributes which have been stated in the Qur'an and explained by the Holy Prophet *s.a.w.*;

3. Belief in His exclusive powers which emanate from His attributes; and

4. Acceptance of such rights exclusive for Him as are integral part of His attributes and a disregard of which renders the belief in His attributes meaningless.

As far as the first of the above conditions is concerned it is self-contained and needs no elucidation. How would a person believe in Allah if he does not believe even in His existence.

The other three conditions are not so clear and require clarification. It seems, therefore, necessary to discuss them at length. In this connection it would be relevant to mention the attributes of Allah and their implications. The position of all His attributes is not the same. Among them such attributes as are of key-importance are only a few or in a way one only. All His other attributes are integral part of it, or its logical results. We think that if the necessary details in regard to it are brought forth there would be no need to amplify here His other attributes. What attributes do we expect of Allah for our belief in Him? The whole matter will become clear as we answer this question. Keeping this in view, we would confine our discussion to

13

only some of His basic attributes and their implications.

Following are the basic and some of the more important attributes of Allah.

1. He is the Eternal, the Everlasting and the Self-existing. It means that He has always been and shall always be. Nobody has created Him. He exists of His own.

2. He is the Creator of everything. It means that He creates things and brings them into existence from nothingness.

3. He is the Lord (the Sustainer). It means He provides food to everyone and sustains everything.

4. He is the King and the Ruler and each and everything is owned by Him and is subservient to Him.

5. He is the Knower. It means that He knows everything, every action and every movement. What has happened, what is happening and what will happen, everything is in His knowledge. Nothing is beyond His ken.

6. He is the Wise. It means that none of His action lacks wisdom, purpose and result. Every action of His has the highest degree of wisdom, prudence and purpose behind it.

7. He is the Mighty. It means that He has the power to do every-thing. None of His intentions can be stopped from mater-ialisation.

8. He is the Just. Every action of His is based on justice and fair-ness. All His injunctions, inherent as well as religious, are just. All His decisions are consonant with justice.

9. He is the Competent. He rewards people according to their actions. He punishes them for their misdeeds and gives good reward for their good deeds.

10. He is the Worshipped. He descries that we worship Him,

prostrate before Him and address all our prayers, longings and supplications to Him.

11. He is the One. It means that in all His attributes no one is His competitor or sharer. Not only is he the Eternal, and the Everlasting, the Creator and the Sustainer, the Kind and the Ruler, the Knower and the Wise, the Mighty and the Just, the Competent and the Worshipped, but that He and He alone is such.

Among the attributes of Allah enumerated above, the attribute of Unity, mentioned towards the end, has a special and distinctive position. As the articles of faith are the soul of Islam, similarly the essence of these articles of faith is the firm belief in the Unity of Allah. If we carefully consider this attribute of Allah, we will find that it is the culmination of all of His other attributes. Therefore this one represents and substitutes His other attributes. He who says with consciousness and conviction that Allah alone is to be worshipped, in fact he declares his firm faith in all the attributes of Allah. If we keep in view this distinctive and comprehensive character of the attribute of Unity, it no longer remains necessary to dilate upon the implications of His other attributes separately. It would be sufficient to discuss the implications of this attribute only. The illustrious Qur'an and the sayings of the Messenger of Allah reveal that the essential implications of this Unity are as follows:

1. There is no other being except Allah, Who has come to exist by His own virtue. Everything else is creation and has been created by Allah:

Allah is the Creator of all things (39: 62).

Everything belongs to Him, is dependent on Him, is subservient to Him:

He is the One, the Omnipotent (13: 16).

Things of the universe do not have any quality of their own;

whatever quality is found in anything, is bestowed upon it by Allah and can remain in it only as long as He desires.

2.   Allah is basically different from all other beings and there is no one at all similar to Him:

Naught is as His likeness (42: 11).

He is beyond imagination as He cannot be compared with the greatest of being:

Allah is the Sublime Similitude (16: 60).

He is neither a father of any one nor anyone's child:

He begetteth not nor was begotten (112: 3).

Neither He integrates Himself with anyone nor anyone ingresses in Him.

3.   It is to please Allah alone that one should be concerned about. This and this alone should be the motive and ultimate goal of all his actions.

4.   All actions and movements which, either in appearance or reality, have any semblance of worship, should be reserved for Allah. Only unto Him can we bow down in worship. Vows can be taken in His name only. Prayers can only be addressed to him. Unseen protection can be sought of Him only. He alone can be called for invisible help.

5.   All sentiments and feelings as are in the spirit of worship should be specified for Allah. Hopes should be linked with Him only. He alone should be feared. The real love should be for Him only.

6.   Allah is the Supreme Ruler of this universe, of which this world of ours is also a small part. He alone has the right to command, to forbid and to subjugate. He is the real Law-Giver and Law-Maker. He alone holds the entire power to designate a man's role in life, to adjudicate his affairs and to forgive or punish him.

7.   No one but Allah possesses the glory of being the One and Only Creator to be worshipped. He alone deserves adoration. His pleasure alone is worth seeking. There is no one else unto whom bowing down in prayer is justified and whose beneficence deserves gratuitous acknowledgement. There is no one except Allah who should be considered a friend, a redeemer of difficulties, a provider of needs and a rescuer from troubles. There is no one, except Allah, to whom prayers and supplications should be addressed and who should be called for help in adversity. There is no one, except Allah, in whom trust can be reposed and whose fear admitted in our hearts. It is He alone, with whom hopes can be associated and for whom real love may be entertained. No other being holds even an iota of the real power. There is no one except Allah who has the power to do good or harm even on a most infinitesimal scale. There is no one, except Allah, who has a legitimate right of laying down law and enforcing his will on any one and submission to whom without any force or compulsion is justified.

These basic implications of the Unity of Allah are so important that the denial of even one of them renders the claim of faith in Allah meaningless. It means that all these things are included in the very concept of the faith of Unity. No one can be a true Muslim until and unless this faith, with all its implications, is deeply enshrined in his heart.

Ascribing Partners unto Allah

A concept becomes clear in our minds only when its converse is also stated. That is why in the exposition of important principles and concepts usually their opposite notions are stated besides them. The concept of Unity is no exception to it. To make it clearly intelligible it is but necessary that its opposite notion, which ascribes partners unto Allah, is also understood. The Holy Qur'an has provided us with a guideline in its treatment of this subject. While teaching about the Unity of Allah, the Qur'an does not close its discussion on a mere definition if this concept. Nor does it rest content with the arguments, merits and results of this concept. The Qur'an has considered it essential to dilate upon the nature, practices, signs and demerits of its opposite concept, which ascribes partners unto Allah and has also provided answer to the question why such a belief is absolutely false and baseless. So much so that even the technical phrase, used by the Qur'an contains both the affirmation of the Unity and the negation of all notions at variance with this concept. Rather than saying "Allah alone is a Being worthy of worship", it says

There is no god but Allah (37:35).

This manner of expression makes it quite clear that unless the notion which ascribes partners unto Allah is completely negated, an unadulterated concept of Unity cannot emerge. When the negation of an idea is so essential, its knowledge must also be essential.

The Arabic word used for any notion that ascribes partners unto Allah is '*Shirk*' which means "to share". In technical terms it means that in one sense or the other someone is considered a sharer in the Being of Allah and His attributes, or in the implications of His attributes. This ascribing of partner unto Him can be of three types:

First, relating to *His Being.*

Second, relating to *His attributes.*

Third, relating to *the implications of His attributes.*

The common forms of ascribing partners unto Allah are:

1.   Someone is considered of the same kind as Allah.

2.   Someone is considered as His father or His child.

3.   Belief that He has become one by integrating Himself with some being.

4.   Assumption that He appears in the shape of some creature or some creature can be His descendent. For instance, the Arabs considered the angels as God's daughters and the

jinns as His family-folk. Similarly, the Christians regarded Jesus (*a.s.*) as the only son and descendent of God. All this amounted to ascribing partner unto His Being.

The practical form of the second type is the belief that out of the attributes of Allah any attribute is present in someone else also and it is believed in the same sense as it is in Allah. For example, "knowledge" is one of His attributes, which signifies that He knows everything whether it is manifest or secret. For Him that which is actually absent is present. The past and the future are, for Him, the present. If someone thinks that a certain creature also knows everything like Him, it would amount to considering him a partner in the attributes of Allah. Similarly to benefit and to harm is an attribute of Allah, which implies that He provides the source of joy and pleasure to whom He likes and deprives of this whom He so desires. If someone thinks that any angel, jinn or saint can address his misfortune or can trouble and harm him, he will be making him a sharer in one of the attributes of Allah. This will tantamount to partnership in His attributes.

In the third type the imperative implications of His attributes are not considered exclusive for Allah and all or any of His attributes are associated with someone else also. For example, one implication of the attributes of Allah is that the real love and submission is for Allah alone. If a person has a similar love and submission for any one else also and thinks him worthy of the same obedience; he would thereby make him a sharer in the attributes of Allah. The highest power lies in the hands of Allah and the right of command is reserved for Him. If someone else is also given this position, whether it is an individual or a group, it will amount to ascribing partners unto Allah.

In the presence of any of the above-mentioned types of beliefs the Islamic concept of the Unity of Allah ceases to exist. Where the concept of Unity ceases to exist, faith also is undone. And where there is no faith the existence of Islam is out of question. This is why the Qur'an has regarded it "the greatest of the wrongs":

To ascribe partners (unto Him) is a tremendous wrong (31:19).

The Qur'an has expressly stated that "there is forgiveness for every sin except for the sin of ascribing partner unto Allah":

Lo! Allah forgiveth not that a partner should be ascribed unto Him. He forgiveth (all) save that to whom He will (4:48).

There is no alternative here but to admit that nothing more can be fairer than this contention. Metaphorically, it amounts to saying that a tuberculosis patient who has reached the third stage of his disease can be cured by medical treatment but not a person whose heart has stopped beating. Would a tree ever grow where there is no seed?

4

FAITH IN THE AFTERLIFE

Meaning of Faith in the Afterlife

One is required to accept wholeheartedly the following for a faith in the Afterlife:

1.   Man is created with a definite purpose. He is a responsible being. His Creator has given him a complete code of guidance.

Leading a life in accordance with the guidance is righteousness and piety but to adopt a way or one's own liking, without any regard of the Divine guidance, is a deviation from the right path and a sin.

2.   The life of man does not come to an end with his death. It continues after his demise also. During the course of his life whatever he does is finished so far as its material results are concerned, but its moral results still continue. A day will come when in accordance with the wisdom and will of Allah, the whole set up of this universe will be destroyed and no creature will remain alive. All, without any exception, will be subjected to death. In terms of the Qur'an this day is called "Doomsday"

3.   After the "Doomsday" all creatures, who have taken birth and died since the creation of the world till now, as well as those who have still to take birth and die, will again be brought to life (body and soul). This is called "Resuscitation".

4.   After the "Resuscitation" will begin the second period before our life. We will be presented in the court of Allah and He will ask for the account of our first life. The record of our whole life, not excluding even a particle of our virtue or vice, will be placed before us.

The scale of justice will be fixed and actions of every one will be weighed. Such fortunates whose actions will carry weight and whose account will comprise of good deeds, will be awarded in the second life a place which will be full of Divine graces. These Divine graces will be unlimited, everlasting and far beyond our human imagination. After the attainment of this place one shall have desire for nothing. The name of this place is "Paradise"

Such unfortunates, whose case will be contrary to above, and whose record will comprise of evil deeds and who will appear before Allah with a record of sheer negligence and disbelief will be condemned to a place which will be full of unending troubles and torments. The name of this place is "Hell".

5.   When this reckoning will be over and a judgement passed over them the second period of our life will begin in earnest. This period shall be unending, and life there would be for ever. There the name of death will be unknown.

The Importance of the Faith in the Afterlife

It is indispensable for a Muslim to have as much faith in the Afterlife as he has in Allah. Without this he cannot become a true believer. In its absence the faith in Allah becomes meaningless because the Afterlife is actually an implication of the many attributes of Allah i.e., the Justice, the Wisdom, the Kindness, the Recognition of Virtue and the Supremacy.

In the absence of the concept of resurrection and reward, our faith that the Creator of this universe is the Just, the Wise, the Merciful, the Recogniser of virtues, the Supreme and the Lord becomes meaningless. In this world very often the moral consequences of our actions do not come forth as they should. Frequently the aggressors prosper while the righteous suffer hardships. If in the Afterlife there does not come an opportunity when every one will get due reward for his actions, it will result in a situation which would negate the Justness, the Wisdom, the Compassion and the Supremacy

of Almighty Allah. As such belief in Allah and disbelief in the
reward and retribution may coexist in words but there is no
possibility of their coexistence in reality.

The Unbeliever's Concept of Intercession

In the Afterlife, a decision as to who led the life of a believer
(Muslim) and in reward thereof be given a place in Paradise, will lie
in the hands of Allah:

The Sovereignty on that day will be Allah's (22:56).

So, from whatever rational angle this matter is viewed the
following conclusions are unavoidable:

1. Allah is the Owner and the Ruler of the whole universe. Hence,
    no reason why the authority of decision should-be in the hands
    of any one other than Allah.

2. He is the Knower. Everything, from the beginning of this world
    to eternity, is in His direct knowledge. What has been done by
    a person in this world, what his hands have earned, what his
    heart's desires have been, what sentiments he nourished in his
    bosom, how he spent the dull darknesses of nights and how he
    spent the busy hours of day, all these things will be as open to
    Him as the sun which shines at midday before our eyes. In view
    of this fact He cannot be dependent on anyone for arriving at a
    correct decision. Nor does He stand in need of any one's advice,
    opinion or evidence. More so, where this "anyone" would not
    even be of the kind who has a correct knowledge of his own
    past and future, how is it possible that with a far lesser
    knowledge, or rather no knowledge, will he be able to assist
    Him in arriving at a correct decision who has full knowledge?

3. He is the Just. By virtue of this attribute it is not possible that
    on the intercession of someone He would forgive even those
    who, as a matter of principle, do not deserve to be forgiven on
    account of their default in faith or in action it would not be in

keeping with His Justness.

In short, from whatever angle one may see there is no room for any sort of wishful thinking that success in the Afterlife depends upon the pleasure of some saint rather that on one's own faith and actions and that their intercession will get the sinful pardoned by influencing the judgement of Allah, even if under the law of chastisement they do not deserve to be pardoned. The Glorious Qur'an decrees all such presumptions baseless and declares in unambiguous terms that no such intercession will be of any avail. In fact, no such intercession will be possible at all.

Expend of that which we have bestowed upon you ere the Day comes wherein there will be neither bargain, nor friendship nor intercession (2:254).

Therefore, the idea of such intercession is altogether baseless. A deeper consideration would reveal that in its character it is an idea of the unbelievers. This idea can only be accepted when it is presumed that Allah is neither the Supreme nor is He above the intervention of someone in making decisions about His subjects, nor His knowledge encompasses everything, nor is He the just. Obviously, only an unbeliever can have such ideas about Allah, not at all a Muslim.

Islamic Concept of Intercession

It does not, however, mean that there will be no intercession, whatsoever, in the Afterlife. The fact is that the Qur'an and the Traditions have repeatedly contradicted the unbelievers idea of intercession. But, nevertheless, they have provided a clear proof of a particular concept of intercession. This concept constitutes a part of the detail of articles of faith and holds that on the day of the Judgement some persons will intercede for others.

What kind of intercession will it be, can it be anticipated to some extent? Obviously, it will not be of the kind already discussed. There will be a fundamental difference between the two. It will be of the kind which will not make it obligatory to disbelieve any of the attributes of Allah or any implication thereof. It will not be in conflict with the established truths that Allah is the Owner and the Ruler of the entire universe, He knows everything and all His works and decisions are weighed in the scale of Justice. If all these things are explicitly understood this intercession will not remain so simple and unqualified. It will be rather of a special kind, limited, qualified and subject to certain rule and principle.

The Glorious Qur'an has not only endorsed the above mentioned presumption but has also explained the details of the rules and principles, under which this intercession will be made. They are as follows:

1. The intercession will be completely in the hands of Allah Himself and nothing would happen without His Will:

    Say: unto Allah belongeth Intercession (39:44)

2. Those permitted by Him alone shall put in a word for others:

    Who is he that intercedeth with Him save by His leave (2:255).

3. The intercessor will intercede only for whom he will be allowed by Allah:

    And they cannot intercede except for him whom He accepteth (21:28).

4. In his intercession he will only say things which will be right in every respect.

    Saving him whom the Beneficent alloweth and who speaketh right (78:38).

It is quite obvious that the intercession will be within the limits stated above. It would not be anything different from a humble petition, supplication, prayer and repentance. The intercessor shall neither add anything to the knowledge of Allah in regard to the faith and deeds of any person nor shall he give his views regarding someone's worthiness for pardon, nor shall he think of influencing the decision of Allah. With His permission he will make a submission unto Allah, the Lord of the Universe, and beg for His Compassion and Mercy. He will pray: "My Lord, I pray Thee to forgive the sins of that servant of Yours, overlook his omission and enfold him in Your compassion and forgiveness."

In fact, as the acceptance of intercession will lie with Allah, the real intercessor will also be Allah. The Qur'an has made this point clear at several places. For instance:

For whom there is no protecting friend nor intercessor beside Him (6:51).

Who will be these intercessors and on whose behalf will they plead? The Traditions reveal that the intercessors will be pious men and favourites of Allah. Who are they going to plead for? They will be such whose weight of faith and deeds will lack some substance and so while reckoning, under the general rule, they will not deserve forgiveness. They will be lacking something for pardon. The intercession will be done to make up the shortfall.

Here arises the question of the significance of the intercession. What would really be the purpose of the intercession? If the intercessor will be as helpless as has been indicated in the verses of the Qur'an referred to above, then Allah must have predetermined their forgiveness, whom he will openly forgive after the intercession? The answer to this question is simple. By the acceptance of their intercession Allah would grace such persons with honour who will have on that Day His permission to speak and submit petitions to Him. On the Day of Judgement when every one present will be dumbfounded, overawed and afraid to look up and when no one will dare to speak, it will be a great honour and distinction for them to intercede. In addition it would be even more meritorious on their part to pray to Allah for the forgiveness of certain persons who would be short of good deeds. The Lord of the Universe will grant their prayers and announce the forgiveness of these persons.

It is abundantly clear from the above that intercession is the name of a particular Divine principle of forgiveness, slightly different from the normal principle of forgiveness. We can regard it as a principle of concession. Nevertheless, this principle is fully consonant with such attributes of Allah as the Unity, the Justice, the Supremacy, the Knowledge and the Honour. It does not in any way infringe His code of reward and punishment.

The Qur'an and the Tradition make it quite plain that in the Afterlife the forgiveness of people would not be possible without His Compassion and Mercy. There is a saying of the Prophet *s.a.w.* that no one will be able to get salvation by dint of his deed alone. *(Muslim)*

This view of salvation is true beyond any doubt. But it is also equally true that His Compassion and Mercy will be in accordance with a certain principle of justice. It will enfold on ly such persons who would really deserve it. The Divine graces will be proportionate to the quality of one's deeds. The better the quality of deeds the greater would be the likelihood for His Compassion and Mercy. He who will have a lesser number of good deeds would stand a lesser chance of His Compassion and Mercy. So much so that a very large number of persons may not be eligible for it. In short, the salvation in the Afterlife would actually depend upon one's own faith and deeds but all decisions in this regard would be entirely in the hands of Allah.

This is the concept of intercession in Islam. Belief in the Afterlife does not make any sense unless the true Islamic concept of intercession is accepted and the mind is purged of all the false notions pertaining to it. As long as the false ideas of inter ession remain in vogue the faith in the Unity of Allah would be meaningless. Belief in Allah and the Afterlife meant that one should possess the knowledge of the truth. It would enable him to follow the right course in practical life and to turn himself into an obedient and true servant of Allah. The unbeliever's concept of intercession hampers the truth. It leads one astray. It keeps him obsessed with the wishful thinking that success in the Afterlife depends not upon one's own faith and good deeds but on the pleasure and intercession of saints and sages which can be acquired by offering vows and oblation to them. Such a notion detracts from the obedience of Allah and fear of the Afterlife. It is an idle fantasy. With it one's entire belief is undone. It is but imperative that one's mind is quite clear about the nature of intercession, if the Islamic concept of the Afterlife is to be understood in its correct perspective.

5

FAITH IN THE PROPHETHOOD

Need for Prophethood

The third article of faith in Islam is Prophethood. In Arabic the word used for it is "*Risalah*" which literally means "Apostleship". In technical terms it means the office of an apostle or Prophet who is sent by Allah to mankind to convey His religious injunctions. Another name for the Prophethood is "*Nubuwah*".

Why was the chain of Prophethood established, how did its need arise and why is it essential to have faith in it? For the consideration of these questions we shall have to go a little into detail. First of all we shall have to see what could be the practical form of fulfilling the aim for which man was created?

The aim of man's creation and the responsibility assigned to him by Islam is that he should worship Allah and submit to Him. Man's happiness in the Afterlife depends on the fulfilment of this aim. The very mention of worship and submission to Allah brings to our mind the question of His injunctions and pleasure. Submission is made to injunctions. In the absence of injunctions we cannot think of Him. As soon as a man decides to live a life of an obedient and submissive servant of Allah, he becomes curious to know the injunctions of his Master which he is required to obey. He becomes anxious to know what pleases Him and what displeases Him. He is keen to learn what he should do for being regarded as His faithful servant and what he should abstain from to avoid the punishment for his disobedience. Without knowing this he would not be able to take even a single step on the path of submission to Allah.

The question naturally arises as to how can we come to know of His injunctions and will? How can we discover what Allah has enjoined upon us and what has He forbidden to us?

One possible means of ascertaining it is our reason. But this will not do. Human beings are not capable of it. There will be nobody who can possibly, with the help of his reason alone, discern his own and the universe's truths. He cannot find out what attributes his Creator and Nourisher has. What are the implications of these attributes in regard to men? What are His commandments? In short, the shortcomings of reason in this respect are beyond any doubt.

The second possible means can be one's own intuition and will power. But this second choice also is not much better than the first. The most vigorous efforts of self-effacement cannot help to attain this objective. However much one may purify his inner-self, he cannot see His injunctions and will reflect in the mirror of his heart. If a mirror is to reflect anything it is not enough that it should be clean and glossy. It is also necessary that what is to be reflected should be exposed and close to it. Until and unless Allah Himself determines and describes His injunctions and infuses them in one's heart, it will not reflect the commandments of Allah in spite of all its purification. But no one has ever made a claim that Allah has devised this system of communicating His injunctions and pleasure. Therefore, this also is a very unworkable way of knowing the Divine injunctions.

The third means of knowing the injunctions and pleasure of Allah is a collective contemplation as against the individual contemplation. As a multitude of blind men unitedly cannot attain the position of somebody whose vision is unimpaired, similarly that crowd of men will not be able to know the injunctions of Allah. It will consist of individuals who, none of them, even individually will be capable of knowing the Divine injunctions with the help of reason. This is why this means of knowledge is as imperfect as the other two mentioned above. So it would not be wrong to say that none of these three means can fulfil this need of man.

There is no denying the fact that in many cases we can ourselves distinguish the good from the bad and on these occasions we are led by our intellect, reason or intuition. Divine guidance is in fact nothing but defining the good and the bad. But it would not be right to infer that since man is able to distinguish a small number of things he is also capable of knowing the Divine injunctions. Knowledge of small number of things does not entitle one to the knowledge of all things. A cursory glance at the world would show that there is no uniformity of opinion about the values of life. There are not many things which are accepted as good or bad universally. Even a lenient view would not help make a long list of such things. A close exami- nation of this list will be still more disappointing as this consensus is further diminished when we go into the detail of these things. Obviously, we cannot make such a tall claim on so slender an evidence. If mankind can decide about a small number of things it does not furnish us with any guarantee that it is also competent enough to solve the entire problem of good and evil. Candle-light no doubt illuminates but it can never replace the Sun which lightens up the entire globe.

The helplessness of man in this respect is admitted on all hands. Neither reason can deny nor intuition challenge it. Such a situation calls for Divine guidance. On the one hand man's reason and intuition were incapable of knowing the Divine injunctions, on the other hand his need for them was as pressing as that of food and drink. In these circumstances there was no alter- native. Some external arrangement had to be made by Allah for his guidance.

So on the one side was the helplessness of man and his most fundamental need for Divine injunctions, on the other side was His Lordship, His Mercy, His Justice and His Wisdom. Every implication of these attributes necessitated that man should not be left to grope in the dark but indeed he should be helped and clearly taught those Divine injunctions without which he could not travel the path of submission and obedience. How was it possible that Allah, the Lord of the Worlds, would not make an external arrangement for communicating His injunctions to men? He would not have delayed it by a day even. It would be rather unbecoming on His part to make such and yet ignore his moral and religious ones. Allah entrusted man with the responsibility of following the path of righteousness. It was beyond His Justice and Mercy to omit necessary arrangements for his guidance. He did arrange for it and in technical terms this arrangement of His is known as "Prophethood". A person through whom this arrangement is done is called "Prophet".

It is abundantly clear that man cannot learn Divine injunctions without the Prophethood. It is also equally clear that the faith in the Prophethood is absolutely essential to be a Muslim, as essential as you need a pair of eyes before you can see anything. If there is only one way that leads to a particular destination one cannot reach it unless he adopts that way.

This matter does not end here. The practical importance of the Prophethood is even more clear-cut. In the absence of Prophethood we would even fail to know Allah and Afterlife, what to say of Divine guidance. It is the medium that provides us with the knowledge of both. To put it more explicitly, without faith in the Prophethood one cannot have faith in Allah and Afterlife, to the required extent. If belief in Prophethood is considered one of the fundamental articles of the faith, it really deserves to be so regarded.

It now stands established that Prophethood is as essential for man as food and drink and belief in it also constitutes a fundamental article of the faith. Now we can go into its details. The important revelations made by the Qur'an in this respect are as follows:

All the Prophets were human

Allah has always chosen men for the communication of His guidance to men. These messengers were neither angels nor jinns nor of any other species. Nor has it ever happened that Allah came unto men in the shape of man or any other form. Whenever a Prophet was sent he was a human being. Allah says:

> *We sent not before thee (any messengers) save men whom we inspired* (12:109).

The events of nations and religions narrated in the Qur'an reveal that the Prophets of Allah were disbelieved by their opponents on the ground that they were similar to them. They enquired how could anyone make a claim of Prophethood if he is a man like others.

> *They said : You are but men like us* (14:10).

No Prophet ever contradicted them on this point. Nor did anyone of them say that he was not like other men. Indeed all of them admitted that they were like other human beings:

> *Their messengers said unto them: We are but men like you* (14:11).

So it is a fact that the Prophets were always appointed from mankind. Like us they had bodies and souls powers and desires. They had wives and children. They were born and bred under the natural laws. They ate and drank, slept and woke, laughed and wept, felt happy and grieved, become hale and hearty or sickened and died like other men. In short they were similar to other men in every respect and had in them all the characteristics of mankind. The details of this fact are disclosed in this verse:

> *We are but men like you* (14:11).

And numerous other verses of the Qur'an also corroborate this fact, i.e.,

> *They ate food and walked in the market* (25:20).

> *We appointed for them wives and offsprings* (13:38).

The consideration which led to the appointment of Prophets out of men is also indicated in the Qur'an. Those who objected to the Prophethood of Muhammad *s.a.w.* said that if Allah were to send His

messenger to them He would have sent an angel and not someone
who was similar to them. In reply to this Allah revealed:

> *Say: If there were in the earth angels walking secure, we had*
> *sent down for them from heaven an angel as messenger* (17:95).

This verse reveals a prescribed Divine Rule for the Prophethood.
It lays down that a Prophet should be from the prime species unto
whom he is sent as a Messenger. Apparently this is a simple phrase
but it is so rich in wisdom that reason stands but convinced of its
veracity. If Prophets wore not appointed from mankind the very aim
of Prophethood would have been frustrated. It is true beyond any
doubt that Prophet is a messenger of Allah to men. It does not,
however, mean that he is akin to a postman and his only task is to
communicate messages like the telephone and telegraph wires. He
is a messenger no doubt but over and above that he is a preacher, a
guide, a teacher and an interpreter. He works for the moral improve-
ment of society through precept and practice. He is the first to
follow the Divine injunctions and sets a pattern of conduct worthy of
imitation. All this constitutes a part of his mission. Unless he
performs all these functions, the purpose for which the chain of
Prophethood is established will not be fulfilled. Can it be possible for
any one except a Prophet to perform all these functions? Obviously
the answer is in the negative. It may be possible for a person to do
it partially but no one will carry out the entire mission assigned to a
Prophet. For instance take the case of angels. They are the first we
can look up to for this purpose. If an angel were sent unto men as
Prophet, what would have been the situation? He would have
conveyed the message of Allah to men but being an angel how could
he follow the injunctions which pertain to the sentiments, desires and
specific problems of mankind? As he would be unable to follow the
greater part of the Divine injunctions, how could he set an example
worthy of imitation. Owing to his ignorance of the sentiments and
desires of mankind how could he provide timely guidance to them?
How could he solve their problems? How could he furnish the details

of the scheme of life enunciated by a Divine Book? Being ignorant of man's self what could he do for its purification?

According to the Qur'an every Prophet was raised from that very nation unto whom he was sent as a messenger of Allah. Similarly the Divine revelation was also in the same language which was spoken by that people:

We never sent a messenger save with the language of his folk (14:4).

Why it was so? To make the Divine message clear to them:

That he might make the message clear for them (14:4).

This statement of the Qur'an will give an idea of how perfect an arrangement was made by Allah to make His message absolutely clear to men. Highest importance has been attached to the fact that nothing should obstruct a clear understanding of the Divine guidance and the logic behind it. It was essential for Prophet to belong to the nation unto whom he was sent as a messenger of Allah. It was also essential for the Divine message to be in the same language which was spoken by that nation unto whom it was delivered. It was still more essential for a Prophet to be a human being among human beings.

Nature of Prophethood

Prophethood is not something which can be acquired by effort. It is bestowed by Allah and is His special gift. It is bestowed upon them only whom Allah chooses for this purpose. Man's effort or intention has nothing to do with it.

Allah Himself chooses persons for this office. In the Qur'anic terminology it is called "*Istafa*" which means to choose the best out of a large number of things. This word denotes that persons chosen for Prophethood were most suitable for this great and sacred mission on account of their multifarious qualities. Its importance appeals to reason. This criterion for choosing a Prophet also seems logically important. The Qur'an has also made it clear in certain verses. When the Prophethood of Muhammad *s.a.w.* was criticised by his opponents and they claimed equal rights for themselves, Allah made it plain to them:

Allah knoweth best with whom to place His message (6:125).

Not only is Prophethood unattainable through effort and learning, its real significance is also beyond our perception. The Qur'an says to this effect:

They will ask thee concerning the spirit. Say: the spirit is by command of my Lord, and of knowledge ye have been vouchsafed but little (17:85).

It means that knowledge and perception or man are so constituted that it is beyond his power to understand the spirit and its reality. Inability to understand the spirit actually means inability to understand the Prophethood. In fact this is the essence of Prophethood. He who gets it becomes a Prophet.

Universality of Prophethood

Prophets have been sent to every nation.

And there is not a nation but a warner hath passed among them (35:24).

This is how it should have been. The reason is that men all over the world are equal. They have been created with one purpose. submission to Allah is the aim of every one. In the Afterlife every one shall be asked to account for it. This being the situation, would it make sense if Allah were to remind only some of this duty and ignore the rest? How could it be that while His guidance was given to certain groups of men, others were left out? This could never happen because He is the Creator, the Master and the Lord of all discrimination. His mercy is common to all and His justice is immune from every kind of bias or favour.

It maybe noted here that when we claim that a Prophet was sent to every nation it means that he was sent in a certain generation of a nation.

Position of Prophet's Teachings

Whatever is taught by a Prophet to men is on Allah's behalf. He says nothing on his own:

> *Nor doth he speak of (his own) desire. It is naught save an inspiration that inspired* (53:3.4).

When it is said that whatever a Prophet teaches is on behalf of Allah, it has a wider meaning. These teachings are of two types:

> Teachings of the first type are those which Allah conveys direct or through some angel to His Messenger in precise words. Teachings of the second type are those precepts which a Prophet deduces from Divine injunctions taught or revealed to him.

The first type of teachings are original and direct from Allah while the latter are indirect and deduced by a Prophet but nevertheless they are Divine for all intents and purposes.

Innocence of Prophets

Prophet is innocent. He errs neither in perception and deduction, nor in action and conduct. His passions, conduct, thoughts and deeds are proof against all kinds of evil influences. He is liable to err in matters outside the domain of religion but such things do not in any way impair his authority. His innocence denotes that he makes no mistake in understanding Divine injunctions or deducing further precepts from them nor does he commit any negligence in their actual practice. This is why his vulnerableness in other matters does not reflect upon his innocence.

Prophet is not innocent for the reason that he does not have the

ability to think or do wrong. The actual position is quite otherwise.
Like all men, Prophets s.a.w. are also liable to make mistakes. But
this fallibility on a Prophet's part never gets a chance because his
thinking and vision are as perfect as his moral. On the one hand he
is best able to understand the purpose of Divine injunctions and draw
further precepts from them. On the other he has full control over his
own self. His moral sense, fear of Allah and the thought of Afterlife
are so powerful that he does not feel any urge for a sin.

But this is not the only reason for the innocence of Prophets.
What really elevates them to the high position of innocence is Divine
supervision. In fact it is this supervision which saves them from
every intellectual and moral default. It would not be correct to say
that a Prophet does not err at all. He is certainly liable to err and
sometimes he actually does. But whenever this happens he
immediately gets a warning from Allah, and before other people can
come to know of it, it is set right by means of a Divine inspiration.
Whenever he feels an urge for a sin his own moral power crushes it.
In the encounter with evil his moral strength is not alone, it is
accompanied by Divine help which curbs it so strongly that no trace
of such an urge is left in him.

The innocence of Prophet was but essential for the mission for
which the chain of Prophethood was established. How could anyone
expect people to believe that his claim to Prophethood was just when
they had a constant suspicion that he could tell a lie, fall a prey to
some base urge and make a wrong interpretation of Divine
injunctions? How could people be sure that such a person was really
conveying to them the guidance of Allah and had not fabricated the
whole thing? Such a person could not present a pattern of conduct
worthy of imitation because he whose own character is not above
board cannot justifiably advise others for an exemplary conduct.

Prophethood would utterly fail in its mission if a Prophet does
not present a perfect example of complete submission and obedience
to Divine injunctions before his followers.

Not only is a Prophet innocent but he alone is innocent. Immunity from intellectual as well as physical errors is only the speciality of these blessed ones of Allah. Others cannot attain it however accomplished in the perception and practice of religion they may be. Thoughts and deeds of a person may touch the fringes of innocence but it is altogether impossible that his perception become immune from error and that whatever he thinks is an absolutely correct interpretation of Divine injunctions.

The last point of this discussion has a special relevance. If the fact that no one except a Prophet is innocent is not firmly rooted in one's mind, he cannot love and submit to a Prophet to the extent required and in consequence may be led to the sin of associating partners unto a Prophet.

Position of Prophets

Complete submission and obedience to Prophet is absolutely essential. To believe so is a prerequisite of faith. In matters of religion and Divine law whatever a Prophet says is to be complied with by his followers without demur. Whether or not they understand its implications, they must believe that whatever a Prophet says is nothing but good and true. This position of Prophet has been determined by Allah Himself:

We sent no messenger save that he should be obeyed by Allah's leave (4:64).

This obedience and submission to the commandments of a Prophet should not only be verbal. It must be sincere and wholehearted. Concerning the obedience of the last Prophet Muhammad *s.a.w.* Allah says:

But nay, by the Lord, they will not believe (in truth) until they make thee judge of what is in dispute between them and find within themselves no dislike of that which thou decidest, and submit with full submission (4:65).

It was but essential. Any concept of Prophet, except the one mentioned above, would not be rational. Since man has been created for the submission and obedience of Allah, and the Prophet is a source for learning its ways and means, one must follow him earnestly and completely. If it is true that a person cannot reach a destination without travelling a path that leads to it; and if one cannot make an air-journey without an aeroplane, then it is equally true to say that a person cannot follow the guidance of Allah unless he abides by the preachings of a Prophet. The Qur'an reveals that whenever a Prophet made a declaration of his Prophethood he demanded from people: "So fear Allah, and obey me" (26:126).

In fact this is a revelation of the truth that the path of obedience and submission can be discovered by following him only. He alone can tell what the injunctions of Allah are and how we should act upon them. This is why Allah has not only ordered submission to Himself but also enjoined obedience to the Prophet.

The fact that whatever a Prophet says in regard to the religion and Divine injunctions is entirely on behalf of Allah, makes this position of the Prophet all the more important. Obedience to him is actually obedience to Allah. "Whoso obeyeth the messenger obeyeth Allah" (4:80). Therefore if the submission to someone is as good as submission to Allah he is worthy of an unqualified obedience.

In short it is a prerequisite of faith in Prophethood that one should render complete obedience to a Prophet, obedience which is neither qualified nor superficial. Any underestimation in this behalf would impair one's faith in him. It would be nothing but sheer ignorance of the significance of Prophethood.

Denying of a Single Prophet is also Disbelief

Belief in Prophethood is meaningless unless it covers all the Prophets. The Qur'an does not take them for Muslims who accept some of them as Prophets and reject others:

*Lo! Those who disbelieve in Allah and His messengers, and seek
to make distinctions between Allah and His messengers, and say:
we believe in some and disbelieve in others, and seek to choose
a way in between; such are disbelievers in truth* (4:150-151).

These words unequivocally declare that the denial of even a
single Prophet results in disbelief of the last degree. If one does not
believe in even one of them his belief in all others becomes void. It
appears to be a hard decision but the exigencies of the truth
warranted that the denial of one single Prophet should not be
regarded a sin of lesser degree. Since every Prophet is sent by Allah
and conveys His injunction to men he assumes the position of a ruler
designated by Allah. When someone disbelieves any of the Prophets,
he virtually disobeys the authority of the Lord of the universe. It is
a revolt against Him. In view of this disbelief his faith in the other
Prophets becomes illogical. It is as if a person recognises all officers
of a government as its representative but excludes one of them. In
doing so he would not be faithful to the Government but to his
whim. Such acceptance and obedience has, therefore, no value. They
who go by their whims in this matter are held by Allah as
disbelievers. For instance, concerning the nation of the Prophet
Noah, Allah says:

*And Noah's folk, and when they denied the messengers, We
drowned them* (25:37).

They had in fact denied only one Prophet. The question of other
Prophets was not faced by them.

We have learnt that every Prophet comes to men so that they
should follow him in accordance with the will of Allah. He who
shows obedience to a Prophet indeed shows obedience to Allah. In
view of this position would it be wrong to say that denying of a single Prophet means disregard of the will of Allah and disobedience
of His injunctions? Would it be any thing but disbelief and revolt of
an extreme type? Without believing each and every Prophet of Allah

would a claim of true faith be justified?

The Prophethood of Muhammad *s.a.w.*

The details of Prophethood given above are in the nature of broad principles of this belief and not its exhaustive study. The Islamic concept of Prophethood is not fully explained in this brief account, nor does it suffice for the understanding of its true Islamic concept. The Islamic concept of Prophethood is accomplished and takes its complete and clear shape only when obedience and submission of the last Prophet Muhammad, *s.a.w.*, is considered as essential. It means that in principle one should consider Muhammad *s.a.w.* a Prophet as much as he considers the others and believe in others as much as he believes in him. But in practice one should choose only him and it should be with the certitude that now his obedience alone is essential. All Prophets were the messengers of Allah and so when a person believes in the concept of Prophethood with this precondition, along with its usual and logical features stated above, only then he becomes a true believer of the Islamic concept of Prophethood[1].

---

[1] This special distinction of the Prophet Muhammad *sallallahu alaihi wasallam* has been discussed at length in chapter 14 "Islam and Other Religions".

6

MUSLIM'S FUNDAMENTAL DUTIES
(RELATING TO THE PRACTICAL SIDE OF ISLAM)

Pillars of Islam

Now that the beliefs have been discussed, it would be only natural to turn to the duties enjoined by Islam. Our attention now by itself shifts to Islam's practical aspect and seeks to discover the duties it prescribes for a Muslim. It is a vast subject and thousands of pages would not suffice for its full exposition. However for the purpose of a general introduction it is not necessary to go into minute details. A brief survey of the cardinal injunctions of Islam would be sufficient for our purpose here. Such injunctions can be classified into two categories:

First, injunctions which are of basic importance in the teachings of Islam and in order of priority rank next to beliefs;

Second, injunctions which have a position different from the first category of injunctions and in order of importance come after them.

Obviously such injunctions, the religious importance of which is most fundamental, deserve our attention first.

What could be the duties which Islam has enjoined upon a Muslim? We need not make any speculations or conjectures about them as the Prophet Muhammad *s.a.w.* himself set forth these injunctions. Here is a well-known saying of his to this effect:

"Islam is founded upon five things. Admission that none except Allah is worthy of worship and Muhammad *s.a.w.* is His Prophet, observing of prayers, payment of poor-tax, making pilgrimage and observance of fasting in the month of Ramadan" (*Bukhari*).

In one of the traditions it has been elucidated that after saying the words "Islam is founded upon five things" the Prophet *s.a.w.* used the word (دعائم) also. With the addition of this word, the sentence gives the meanings "Islam is founded upon five pillars." Now, pillars of a building constitute neither a whole building nor are they anything apart from it. Like its other portions, pillars are also a part of it. There is, however, a remarkable difference between the two. Owing to their singular importance in structure, pillars have a distinct position. Unless pillars are completed further construction of a building is not possible. On the same analogy, if these duties of Islam are ignored, the other teachings of Islam cannot be practised either. If anything is done ignoring them it may have the semblance of a duty but it will be certainly void of essence.

The fulfilment of these duties means the fulfilment of the remaining duties as well. That is why in another tradition only these duties have been called "Islam".

"Al-Islam implies that you testify that there is no god but Allah and that Muhammad is the messenger of Allah and you establish prayer, pay zakat, observe the fast of Ramadan, and perform pilgrimage to Holy Ka'aba at Mecca once in a lifetime if you are solvent enough (to bear the expense of) journey".

In the first tradition these duties were designated as the "Pillars of Islam" but being the vital duties they actually cover the whole of Islam.

The fact that these duties being of vital importance cover the whole of Islam will become amply clear in the forthcoming details.

Now let us study the details of these Pillars of Islam which occupy the foremost position in Islam.

Admission of the Unity and Prophethood

Admission of the unity and Prophethood of Muhammad *s.a.w.* is a duty which is executed verbally. It denotes much more than its literal meanings. It signifies admission of all the Prophets, Scriptures, Angels, Afterlife and Predestination. In short, it is admission of all the Islamic beliefs because he who admits the Prophethood of Muhammad *s.a.w.* thereby admits all those unseen realities which he has revealed to us.

To have wholehearted belief in the unity of Allah and Prophethood of Muhammad *s.a.w.* is one thing. To admit this belief and make a verbal declaration of its truth is another. The study of traditions and the commentary of religious scholars reveal that for becoming a Muslim it is not enough that one has a wholehearted faith only. It is equally important that he also makes a verbal declaration of it. In the absence of a verbal declaration one's faith does not become valid. This verbal declaration owes its importance to the fact that Islam is a religion and not a whispering campaign. Its duties are not performed in isolation. It is actually a religion which speaks to mankind aloud. It plants him in the midst of the tumult of life. It keeps him engrossed in a perpetual struggle between good and evil. It places him in the vanguard of an army ceaselessly fighting against disbelief and sin. This situation warranted a declaration from everyone who embraced Islam—a declaration that he was a missionary and a soldier fighting for the cause enjoined by his faith. In view of the above it should be agreed that the declaration of the Islamic beliefs is of paramount importance.

This admission and declaration will appear all the more important if we see it from a political angle. When someone openly affirms his faith in the Unity of Allah and the Prophethood of Muhammad *s.a.w.* he is considered a Muslim, even if he does not really believe it and fails to fulfil its practical implications. After affirming his faith he acquires the rights to which a Muslim is entitled politically and socially. On the contrary, if a person does not make a verbal admission and declaration of it, however much he believes in it, he will not be accepted as a Muslim. He will remain a non-Muslim and treated likewise. If a person wholeheartedly believes in the veracity of Islamic beliefs, he lays a firm foundation for his faith. But if he vehemently believes and also makes an open declaration of it, he completes the construction of its first pillar.

7

PRAYER (Ṣalāt)

Importance of Prayer in Islam

The second pillar of Islam is prayer. It has a pre-eminent position among the practical duties. No other duty approaches its level. Every act of a Muslim is an act of submission but the elegance of prayer surpasses all. It is a submission in appearance as well as in effect. A glance at the form of prayer will prove this assertion. The supplication, the praise and the recitation, which it includes, convince that there is hardly any form of servility and meekness that is not found in the form and essence of prayer. Standing lowly with folded arms, bowing head in gratitude, prostration as a mark of humility and constant utterance of words of magnificence and praise and to be obsessed with the fear, greatness and love of Allah, such are the signs which permeate a prayer. The Qur'an and the tradition are replete with the virtues and pre-eminence of prayer. Of these, a few are enumerated below:

Prayer is the first manifestation of faith. It must have been observed in the traditions quoted above that after the admission of faith the first thing that finds a mention in them is prayer. It is indicative of the fact that if a person has faith and also believes that Allah alone is his Master and he is nothing but a humble slave of His, his belief manifests in prayer. It is not only mentioned in the traditions cited above but almost in every tradition in which the duties of Islam have been enumerated.

Similarly, at numerous places in the Qur'an prayer is mentioned immediately after faith. For instance,

Lo! Those who believe and do good works and establish prayer (2: 277).

And as for those who make (men) keep the scripture and establish worship (7: 170).

For he neither testified nor prayed (75: 31).

It signifies the fact that if the seed of faith is laid in ones heart the first shoot that sprouts will be prayer.

Prayer is not only the first manifestation of faith but in fact a logical outcome of it. One whose heart is brimful of faith, his head is bound to feel an urge for obedience and obeisance. Prayer is in fact the name of an inner condition which finds expression in the form of prayer. Prayer is to faith, what light and heat is to the sun. That prayer is vital to faith is not a mere presumption. It is an express command of the Prophet *s.a.w.* He says:

"He who deliberately neglects an obligatory prayer, Allah is absolved of him" (*Ahmad*).

"Verily, it is prayer which separates man and disbelief to polytheism".

It was laid down by the Prophet *s.a.w.* that in the course of holy war such villages where the call to prayer (*Adhan*) was heard were to be taken for habitations of Muslims, and exempted from attack. On the other hand, any village from where came no call to prayer could be presumed to be a non-Muslim colony and attacked. This principle is an evident proof of the fact that ordinarily prayer serves as a mark of faith. Whether a person is Muslim or otherwise can also be asserted by this mark.

It is stated in the Qur'an that on the Day of Resurrection the angels would inquire from the inhabitants of hell:

What hath brought you to this hell? (74:42)

Their reply would be in these words:

We were not of those who prayed (74:43).

It means that one who establishes prayer is as good as the one who is a believer and has faith in the Unity of Allah. It is an established fact that one's eligibility to heaven and hell depends on his belief and disbelief.

When people condemned to hell will see for themselves the unseen realities, they will confess that their suffering was a sequel to their default in prayer. Does it not establish the fact prayer that on the Day of Resurrection faith and prayer will distinguish and compliment each other. Instead of saying, we were not of those who believed" they will say: "We were not of those who prayed".

On the strength of these verses some of the religious scholars hold that he who neglects prayer wilfully and insists on its negligence is liable to beheading. This punishment is consonant with the principle which awards a similar punishment to one who becomes an apostate.

Another vital significance of prayer mentioned in the Qur'an and verified by the tradition, is that it is the fountainhead of religious passion. It is a guardian of the faith. If prayer is established, obedience of other injunctions will follow. On the contrary, if prayer is neglected, other injunctions will also go by default. Prayer has the same importance in faith as heart has in the human body. If heart has the vigour, the warmth and the vitality, the flow of blood continues to other parts of the body and keeps them alive and active. But if heart looses life and beat, other parts become lifeless and inactive. We find several indications of this significance of prayer in the Qur'an and the Prophet *s.a.w.* has also elaborated it. The tradition quoted above which signifies that Islam is founded upon five pillars, also contains the words: "The pillar of faith is prayer".

"The essence of faith is the admission, (admission of the Unity

of Allah and Prophethood of Muhammad) and its pillar is
Prayer" (*Tirmidhi*).

This is an evident proof of the fact that although poor tax, pilgrimage, and fasting are also pillars of faith in their own right, and the
edifice of faith cannot be completed without them, till prayer has a
distinction of its own. By virtue of its singular position, it is a pillar
of faith all by its own. This is why prayer is said to signify the whole
faith. If it is neglected, faith ceases to exist. In a letter addressed to
his officers, Caliph 'Umar (*r.a.*) once wrote:

"To me the most important of your problems is that of prayer.
One who establishes prayer and does full justice to it, protects
the whole faith and one who loses it, is destined to lose still
more" (*Malik*).

Reason for the vital significance of Prayer

The evidence provided by the Qur'an and the tradition amply prove
the importance of prayer. One would naturally ask why is it so?
Being only one of the five pillars, how is it equal to complete faith?
The answer to this question in fact lies in another question: What is
prayer and what it precisely stands for? The Qur'an says that prayer
is the name of the remembrance of Allah:

Establish prayer for my remembrance (20: 14).

It brings one near to his Master:

Prostrate thyself and get near (unto Allah) (96: 19).

A man is very near to Allah in state of prostration. So much so
that when any one is in prayer "he converses with Him". In prayer
one is completely cut off from everything, feels himself in "His
presence" and converses with Him.

To remember Him, to be near Him and to converse with
Him—that is prayer. Is there anything else which deserves to be,
regarded the essence of faith and submission? No, certainly not.

Every act which is done for worshipping Allah is a fruit of faith. The roots of faith get their vitality and nourishment from the remembrance of Allah. The faithful are advised to refresh their faith by constant repetition of the words:

"*Lā ilāhā ill-Allāh*" (There is no god except Allah).

"Refresh your faith with the words : Lā ILāHā ILLALLāH: (There is no god except Allah)" (*Bukhari*).

If the roots of a tree fail to get freshness and vitality its growth is arrested. It begins to die. Similarly, one whose heart is without the remembrance of Allah, can hardly keep his faith alive. The act of a man, whose faith withers, will be devoid of piety and fear of Allah. An act of piety can only come from a person whose faith is imbued with freshness and vigour which emanates from the remembrance of Allah. Prayer is not only the remembrance of Allah, it is indeed its best, perfect and the most effective medium. That is why piety, and worship of Allah are based on prayer.

This can be explained by an example. A courtier who neither appears before his king, nor shows the respect and honour due to him, cannot be expected to be loyal and obedient. Loyalty and obedience can only be expected from one who will not be careless in the matter of court attendance or slack in showing respect and honour due to the king. It is but obvious that a person who does not come to you, will not be prepared to take any pains for your will and pleasure. He will, of course, never make the least bit of sacrifice. Prayer is attendance in the court of Allah and a manifestation of one's respect and loyalty to Him. One who is not wholeheartedly ready for such attendance and respect, will never obey His injunctions in the vast orbit of life?

Some Supplementary Objects of Prayer

The real importance and elegance of prayer has already been discussed. But prayer has also in its fold a variety of graces. As compared to the real object of prayer such graces are supplementary in character, but nevertheless they have superb value and importance. They play a vital role in the acquisition of true Islamic outlook and mode of life and as such their knowledge is essential. It would be more appropriate to call "supplementary graces" as "supplementary objectives". Some of them are as follows:

1.   Islam infuses all its followers with one mission. For this purpose it is but imperative that they lead a well disciplined collective life. They have a leader who adheres to the Divine injunctions and makes the whole society follow his example. He should enforce the Divine Injunctions. Under his leadership people act as a disciplined and well-trained army. When he orders them to move they should move and when he bids them to stop they should stop. This is the kind of discipline which prayer inculcates. When they are called to prayer, people leave their houses, workshops and fields and set out for the mosque. Here they stand up in straight rows and meticulously follow the person who is leading the prayer. It is impossible for anyone in that congregation to show any disregard to the leader mentally or physically. All this is done in obedience to the Divine injunctions, religious orders and in the interests of Afterlife. Is it possible to impart mental and practical training in discipline in any other way than prayer?

2.   Islam also likes to see a firm bond of love and fraternity among its followers. Islam lays it down as a mark of true believer that he should like for his Muslim brother what he likes for himself. Prayer creates and fosters this sense of love and fraternity. When the residents of a locality assemble before Allah for prayer they are in love not only physically but spiritually also. It is not merely their shoulders and feet which touch but their hearts also beat in unison. They do not only pray for themselves but beseech guidance, help and forgiveness for all. Is there any better way of loving mankind than this one? One does not forget his follow being even in his humble supplication and prayers to Allah and constantly prays:

Show us the straight path (1:5).

Our Lord! Give unto us in the world that which is good and in the Hereafter that which is good and guard us from the doom of fire (2:201).

The loftiest concept of human fraternity falls short of the standard which Islam has ordained for its followers.

3.   Islam regards all men as bondmen of one Master. It considers the whole mankind as children of one parentage and enjoins to treat all men accordingly.

"O servants of Allah, you should become brothers" (*Bukhari and Muslim*).

Islam ordains that no one should consider any of his fellow beings inferior to himself. It exhorts that nobody is high or low because of his colour, country, race, parentage or wealth. Piety and fear of Allah are the merits for superiority.

The Holy Prophet *s.a.w.* said:

"Man's superiority depends upon his religiousness and piety."

Prayer invokes the consciousness of this reality through its mode and moral. In this way prayer eliminates all distinctions of rank and race. Kings and slaves stand at equal footing and bow their heads alike to their Master. This is a manifestation of equality in the mode of prayer. On the spiritual level it makes all men equal. The greatness of Allah and the utter humbleness of mankind permeates their minds in equal degree. Everyone feels that to Allah, and Allah alone belongs all kinds of greatness. No one is more than a bondsman and slave of Allah. Obviously, if prayer keeps a person so deeply conscious of his humbleness and servitude he will never be deluded by the glint of colour, caste and wealth. Nor shall he ever arrogate to himself any kind of superiority over other follow beings.

Real Prayers

We have discussed above some of the real objectives of prayers and
saw a glimpse of the graces it bestows. Let us now proceed to
discover the real prayer which has been enjoined by Islam. Everyone
who has the appearance of a man is not a man in the real sense,
similarly everything which has a semblance of prayer is not a prayer
indeed. The prayer which has been ordained by Allah and which is
the pillar, or rather the most important pillar of Islam, is not
performed unless it is accompanied by its full decorum. For the
proper performance of prayer the Qur'anic tradition use a special
term *Iqāmat* (اقامت   ) which means "to stand upright". This term
has been used in the tradition cited above and frequently occurs in
the verses of the Qur'an. It denotes that prayer must be performed
with all its external formalities and internal qualities. The details of
these requirements can be easily found in the Qur'an, the book or
traditions and volumes of *Fiqh* (Islamic jurisprudence). Briefly, an
upright prayer is one which is performed at its proper time and in
congregation. It is characterised with grace, discipline and rapt
attention. Recitation is done at a slow pace and all the stages of
prayer standing, bowing, prostration etc. are prolonged. It is a prayer
in which one is full of respect for Allah. It is a prayer in which one
becomes an embodiment of respect and reverence for Allah. Above
all one is totally immersed in the remembrance of Allah and one's
heart is charged with the fear of Allah and one's own humbleness. A
prayer which is full of these qualities will be a prayer in the true
sense of the word. The greater the amount of these qualities, the
higher would be its value. If a prayer does not have even a minimum
of these qualities, it would be a prayer in name and not in spirit. It
will not yield the graces we expect. Such a prayer will not be pillar
of faith, it will be a wall of sand.

The graces emanating from prayer, stated above, have also
another significance. They serve as a gauge for measuring value of
our prayers. We can discover by this means the extent to which we

are keeping our prayers upright. When we have discovered it, we are in a position to evaluate for ourselves whether or not our prayer has attained the significance of pillar of faith? If yes, to what extent ?

8

ZAKĀT (Poor-Due)

Importance of the Poor-Due

The third pillar of Islam is Zakat (Poor-due). As it has already been stated that no act is as important in Islam as the prayer, it would be illogical to say that the position of Zakat in Islam is exactly similar to that of the prayer. But if the injunctions in regard to it given in the Qur'an and the Tradition are kept in view, we shall be led to the conclusion that Zakat ranks next to the prayer. For instance:

1. After making a mention of Faith, the Qur'an frequently mentions two acts of piety, i.e., the prayer and the Zakat. The image of a true Muslim is set forth by the Qur'an usually in words like these:

> *Lo! those who believe and do good deeds and establish prayer and pay the poor-due (zakat), their reward is with their Lord...* (2:277).

When we see that there are other noble deeds which are also essential for a true Muslim, this verse assumes a special significance. While projecting the image of a true Muslim, the Qur'an at first speaks of faith. Why is it that after the Faith, the Qur'an makes a mention of the prayer and Zakat and not of other acts? Why does it not speak of other good acts? Obviously this is not without significance. A thoughtful consideration would make it quite clear. Allah considers the prayer and Zakat as the twin foundation stones of practical faith. If a person performs these two acts properly, he provides a solid guarantee and practical evidence of following the religion in full. Such a person would not be exposed to the danger of neglecting the other injunctions enjoined by faith. Why is it so? Its answer lies in the meaning and purpose of the Faith and the significance of the prayer and the Zakat.

A logical division of the injunctions of Faith would make two categories of them:

First, the injunctions which relate to the rights of Allah on man. Second, the injunctions which relate to the rights of mankind on man.

Thus the practice of the Faith really means that one should acquit himself of the rights of Allah as well as of mankind. From the discussion on the prayer already made and the debate on Zakat that follows, it would transpire that while the prayer is the essence of the rights of Allah, the Zakat is the essence of the rights of men. If a person says his prayer in a mosque, it is unlikely that he would be unmindful of the rights of Allah when he comes out of it. He will discharge these rights with the same constancy as a spring pours out its waters. Similarly, a person who pays Zakat is not likely to transgress the rights of others. One who willingly spends his hard-earned income on his brothers, neighbours and fellow-beings, and by doing so does not wish to earn their gratitude, rather feels obliged to them himself, he would only rest when he has discharged himself of all their rights.

There is another aspect of this issue also. The Qur'an repeatedly exhorts that the Faith becomes a living force only when the love of Allah sways all other attachments and when consideration of Afterlife gets preference over worldly pursuits. The prayer and Zakat are the two most elective means for the attainment of this objective. While the prayer leads one to Allah and the Afterlife, the Zakat inclines him towards the welfare of his fellow-beings. If the pleasure of Allah and success in the Afterlife are like an uphill drive, the prayer and Zakat are the two engines of the train that travels on it. The former engine pulls this train from the front and the latter engine pushes it from the rear. Thus the train of life runs to its destination. When so great is the importance of these two acts, would it be anything but fair if they are real basis of Islam.

2.   When the final order to wage a holy war against the disbelievers of Mecca was given to the Muslims, the Qur'an exhorted not to sheath their swords till the enemies were put to sword or they embraced Islam. For two decades Islam was preached to them and no effort was spared to bring them to the Faith. On this occasion the Qur'an laid down certain conditions on which their faith was to be accepted and the holy war against them stopped. The Qur'an specified:

But if they repent and establish prayers and pay Zakat then leave their way free (9:5).

In a subsequent verse the Qur'an repeats:

But if they repent and establish prayer and pay Zakat then are they your brethren in religion (9:11)

This elaboration makes it quite clear that even after the admission of the Faith the acceptance of Islam was subject to the performance of two acts: namely the prayer and Zakat. As long as one does not acquit himself of both these acts, his faith is not accept-able. It goes to prove that the payment of Zakat is precondition and an insignia of faith. The Prophet *s.a.w.* elucidated this point when he said:

"I have been commanded to fight against people till they testify that there is no god but Allah, and they establish prayer and pay Zakat and if they do it, then blood and property are guaranteed protection on my behalf and their affairs rest with Allah" (*Muslim*).

It was not only for the new Muslims that the Qur'an prescribed the condition of Zakat, it was for all without any exception. If any Muslim refused to pay Zakat, an Islamic government was duty bound to punish him. In the times of the Caliph Abu Bakr (*r.a.*), some of the tribes refused to pay Zakat. He declared war against them. When Umar, the Great (*r.a.*) showed some hesitation in endorsing his action. Abu Bakr (*r.a.*) declared:

"By Allah I would fight definitely against him who makes a distinction between the prayer and Zakat (poor-due) (because they are put together in the Qur'an) (*Muslim*).

This contention was not only accepted by Umar the Great but by all the other companions also (*r.a.*). It leads us to the inference that the life and property of a Muslim deserves respect as long as he performs the prayer and pays Zakat. If a person follows the Divine injunctions in regard to the prayer but tries to avoid the payment of Zakat, and thereby makes a distinction between their position, he would invite upon himself the same punishment which is given to one who neglects the prayer. War is to be declared against him:

And woe unto the polytheists, who give not Zakat, and who are disbelievers in the Hereafter (41:6-7).

Therefore, I shall ordain it (mercy) for those who ward off (evil) and pay Zakat and then who believe in our signs (or verses) (7:156).

It will be observed that while in the former verse non-payment of Zakat is considered at par with disbelief and denial of the Afterlife, in the latter, the payment of Zakat is regarded as a strong evidence of faith and piety. In fact these two verses point towards the truth that Zakat is a must for faith. One who has faith would pay Zakat without fail.

The above mentioned quotations from the Qur'an and the traditions are sufficient to signify the position of Zakat in Islam. They make it abundantly clear that the edifice of Islam cannot be raised without full regard to Zakat. It was actually for this reason that Zakat was included among the Pillars of the Faith.

OBJECTIVES OF ZAKAT (POOR-DUE)

Now we must know the purpose for which Zakat (poor-due) has been made obligatory and what are the objects which are achieved by it. From the study of the Qur'an and traditions of the Holy Prophet it transpires that there are three objects of Zakat, one object is basic and specific and the other two are secondary and collective.

1.   Purification of Soul

The basic and the essential object of Zakat is the purification of soul. It purges the lust of wealth, infuses the fear of Allah in man's heart and makes one amenable to good deeds. The Qur'an says :

Far removed from it (hell) will be the righteous who will give his wealth that he may grow (in purity) (92:17-18).

On another occasion Allah addresses and exhorts the Prophet *s.a.w.* in these words:

Take alms of their wealth, wherewith thou mayst cleanse and purify them (9:103).

These verses make the real importance of Zakat quite clear. It aims to emancipate the heart from the temporal preoccupations and purifies the soul. It is an admitted fact that the love of material things is the real enemy of the prayer. It turns a man away from Allah and the After-life. The Prophet *s.a.w.* once said:

"The root of every evil is the love of worldly things" (*Mishkat*).

Although temporal love includes many things but the most powerful and dangerous of all is the love of the material wealth. The Prophet *s.a.w.* has, therefore, regarded it the greatest of all evils for the Muslims:

"The trial for my *ummah* is wealth". (*Tirmidhi*).

If a Muslim can save himself from the lust of wealth, he will be able to protect himself from many other vices. His release from this bond will practically release him from many others. Emancipation of the heart from temporal love is nothing but its purification. If Zakat yields the freedom of the soul it proves that it has the quality of purifying the soul. Free from the love of worldly things, one strives to seek the pleasure of Allah and the welfare of the Afterlife. He inclines more towards pious deeds. Thus the effect of Zakat is not limited to the process of purification of the heart alone. It makes a more positive contribution, by providing a stimulus for doing good. The quotations mentioned above highlight these qualities of Zakat.

Because of its basic aim and purpose the poor-due is termed as "Zakat" in Islam. Literally it means both "purification and growth". To give a portion of one's income to the needy, for the pleasure of Allah, is called Zakat because it purifies the soul and subscribes to its growth and purification.

It must, however, be remembered that the aim of Zakat is not achieved by paying a portion of income to the poor. It is in fact achieved when its payment is motivated by a sincere desire and practical effort. What is meant by these preconditions is made clear in the Qur'an. A gist of the Qur'anic explanation is given below:

Pre-conditions for purification

Pleasure of Allah

The pleasure of Allah should be the first and foremost consideration while paying Zakat. It must be free from every other motive.

Ye spend not save in search of Allah's pleasure (2:272)

The words "Ye spend not save in search of Allah's pleasure" set forth the principle for the payment of Zakat.

The Qur'an repeatedly says that the mark of a true Muslim is that he pays Zakat and alms for the pleasure of Allah alone. This is why Zakat has also been called an "expenditure in the way of Allah".

Income from honest means

The second important precondition for Zakat is that it should be paid
out of the income earned only by fair and honest means:

*O ye who believe; spend of the good things which ye have
earned (2:267).*

It is further elaborated by the Prophet *s.a.w.* in the Tradition:

*O people, verily Allah is Pure and He does not accept anything
else but pure.*

Only the good things to be paid

The third important pre-condition of Zakat is that whatever is paid
should be of good quality. If cheap and worthless stuff is given in
Zakat, it will go in vain. It will be no better than a hypocritical
gesture.

And seek not the bad (with intent) to spend thereof (in charity)
(2:267).

The recipient's self respect should not be hurt

The fourth pre-condition of Zakat is that its beneficiary should
neither be made to feel grateful for it, nor his feelings and
self-respect hurt. Otherwise Zakat would cease to have any meaning.

*O ye who believe! Render not vain your alms-giving by reproach
and injury, like him who spendeth his wealth only to be seen of
men* (2:264).

A tradition reveals that three persons will enter the hell first.
One of them will be the man who distributed alms to earn the
reputation of being generous and philanthropist. Another tradition
contains a sterner warning:

*He who gives charity to be shown off (by men) he in fact(put
up) rivals (with God) (Mishkat).*

These are the preconditions of Zakat. Strict adherence to them alone will make Zakat a source of piety and purification. What a lofty moral it preaches and how greatly it differs from the ordinary almsgiving. It can be easily concluded from the preconditions that a severe self-examination is of paramount importance while paying Zakat. It is a kind of prayer surrounded by innumerable hostile forces which are always on the ready to give it a fatal blow. In this regard the attitude of the righteous men is specifically mentioned in the Qur'an.

And feed with food the needy wretch, the orphan and the prisoner for love of Him, saying we feed you for the sake of Allah only. We wish for no reward nor thanks from you (76:8-9).

And those who give that which they give with hearts afraid because they are about to return unto their Lord (23:60).

What to say of pride, exultation ostentation, or causing injury to the beneficiary's self-respect, a Muslim is full of fear and awe when he is paying Zakat. The fear and awe that his innerself might have played some mischief on the sly would undo his good deeds. He is afraid that on the day of Judgement, he will appear before Allah, he might find that all his good work in helping the needy has come to naught.

2.   Help of the Poor

Let us now turn to the secondary objectives of Zakat. It provides basic necessities to the poor Muslims. The Prophet s.a.w. said:

"Verily Allah has ordained the payment of Zakat on them (Muslims). It will be taken from the rich and returned to the poor" (*Muslim*).

Similarly, the Qur'an, which regards the payment of Zakat to be a mark of the righteous Muslim, mentions its details in the following words:

And giveth his wealth, for love of Him, to kinsfolk and to
orphans and the needy who ask and to set the slaves free (2:
177).

These quotations make it quite obvious that there is also a social
and economic aspect of Zakat without which its Islamic concept remains incomplete. A person who sets apart a portion of his income for
the poor, undoubtedly arranges for the purification of his soul. Still
this act alone will not suffice for the construction of this pillar of the
Faith. This act will attain its true, objective and subscribe to the
completion of the third pillar of the Faith, only when he would
actually pay that portion of income to deserving men. It is true that
the primary objective of Zakat is the purification of the soul but it is
equally true that unless it serves the needs of the poor, its real
purpose will remain unattained. This duty will be done when the
Zakat will reach their hands. That is the reason why the Qur'an has
regarded Zakat as a right of the poor on the affluent class of the
society.

And in whose wealth there is a right acknowledged for the
beggar and the destitute. (70: 24-25).

This is a right for which an Islamic Government will be prepared even to fight. It is amply illustrated by the instance of the
Caliph Abu Bakr (*r.a.*) cited above. Although this objective of Zakat
is of secondary importance, yet its vital position in Islam cannot be
underestimated. It possesses a superb importance in this world and in
the Hereafter.

The following traditions will give an idea of its prime
importance:

"One who eats to his full appetite while his neighhour starves is
not a true Muslim" *(Mishkat).*

On the Day of Judgement Allah would say: O Sons of Adam, I
asked you for food and you did not give it to me. Man will

reply: "My Lord, how could I provide food to you when You are Yourself the sustainer of all the worlds?" To this Allah would say: "Do not you remember that one of your fellow-beings, who was starving, begged for food and you refused it to him?" *(Muslim)*.

It proves beyond any doubt that Islam is acutely sensitive to the needs of the poor and the destitute. The importance it attaches to the fulfilment of the needs of the poor is something out of the ordinary.

3.   Support of Islam

Among the secondary objectives of Zakat one is the help and support of Islam. While giving, the details of the beneficiaries of Zakat the Qur'an says:

The alms are only for the poor, and the needy, and for those who collect them and those whose hearts are to be reconciled, and to free the captives and the debtors and for the cause of Allah and for the wayfarers (9:60).

The words "the cause of Allah" denote the struggle made for Islam, particularly for meeting the requirements of the holy wars. It clearly means that meeting the financial requirements of the holy war is also an objective of Zakat. In view of this objective the Muslims have been repeatedly exhorted in the Qur'an to this effect:

And strive with your wealth and your lives in the way of Allah (9:41).

When the Qur'an describes the qualities of a righteous Muslim, there is one quality which is invariably mentioned and that is "they wage a war in the cause of Allah with their wealth". Its meanings are quite obvious. It connotes 'that whatever expenditure is to be incurred on holy war, it should be provided by the Muslims from personal wealth.

It is admitted on all hands that the protection and support of religion is not an ordinary matter. As such spending of personal wealth for this purpose has great importance. While enjoining holy war the Qur'an says:

Spend your wealth in the cause of Allah and be not cast by your own hands to ruin (2:195).

It signifies that the non-supply of funds for the protection and support of religion is tantamount to inviting destruction both in this world and in the Hereafter. Something which offers protection from destruction, both in this life and the After-life can never be regarded as a matter of little consequence.

THE QUANTUM OF ZAKAT

After knowing the objectives of Zakat, it would be asked as to what should be the amount of Zakat? The answer is "the amount which is sufficient for the three objectives stated above". On the one side it should purge the heart of the love of wealth. On the other, the scourge of poverty and hunger should be wiped out and the funds required for the protection and security of Islam collected.

Because of the nature of these expenses a fixed scale of Zakat could not be evolved. In a situation like this the best course would be to go on contributing to this noble cause and pay as much as one can. A righteous Muslim does not believe that doing good is more than enough. It is against his religious fervour to be satisfied with any of his pious performances. The Qur'an exhorts the Muslims time and again to spend in the path Allah. This exhortation made such an impact upon the companions of the Prophet (Allah be pleased with them all) that they were not satisfied even with the greatest of sacrifices. For fear of still falling short of their obligation they asked for the fixation of the exact amount they were required to pay:

And they ask thee what they aught to spend (2: 219).

In reply to this they were told to give away everything in the path of Allah that was in excess of their genuine needs

Say: what you can spare (2: 219).

This verse is indicative of the standard required for spending in the way of Allah. It states in clear terms the two secondary objectives of Zakat. It lays down that as long as the individual needs of the poor and the collective requirements of Islam are not fully met the demand on the well-to-do Muslims to spend in the path of Allah will continue. They will not be absolved of this duty even if they have already spent heavily on this account. But ordinarily such a situation hardly arises when it is felt that all the needs of the religion and Muslim Society have been fully met. It means that the well-to-do Muslims will have for ever before them an unending demand for spending in the path of Allah. As long as this demand persists their sense, of duty will urge them to fulfil it and they will never rest content, or feel that they have done all that was required of them. Thus the actual decision as to how much is to be given by way of Zakat and in the path of Allah is left to the religious fervour of the Muslims. Islam is not utopian in character. It is a practical religion and does not dream of ideals which are impracticable. It keeps all the realities of life in view. Like other articles of the Faith, it has not let the question of Zakat to the religious spirit of its followers allowing them to spend to the extent they liked. It has fixed a certain limit of Zakat. This is of course the minimum limit for such objectives of Zakat which make it a pillar of Faith. In the fixation of this limit Islam has kept human needs and experiences fully in view.

As Islam was addressed to each and every class of people including men of different financial status, calibre and abilities, a limit of Zakat seemed but necessary. It was also necessitated by the fact that for the majority of mankind thing defined in exact terms are more suitable than theoretical propositions. They find it easier to comply with an order if it is given with precision and exactness.

Secondly, the religious passion among men is not equal. There are people who have a tendency of capitalising on marginal concessions. This made it necessary to prescribe such minimum limits of the fundamentals of Islam as were imperative for becoming an ordinary Muslim.

Thirdly, the Zakat has not been made obligatory merely for the purification of one's soul. To help the poor and to protect and support the religion are also some of its objectives. So far as the purification of the soul is concerned, it could be left to an individual's own religious zeal. He would pay it if he was prepared to face the consequences of being a defaulter. But since its objectives also include the help of the poor and the protection and support of Islam, and these matters are concerned more with this world than the Hereafter, it could not he entirely left to one's own discretion. It will be wrong to think that Allah has attached so little importance to the material needs of the poor, that He would merely provide incentives and leave this matter to the people. In such a situation the rich would throw some loaves to the starving faction of the society whenever touched by their misery; or they would contribute a few coins for the protection and support of religion; or remain indifferent in either case. These are no doubt the secondary objectives of Zakat yet the importance attached to them by Islam is of a high degree. The very importance implied that this matter was not to be left to the whims and moods of the people. It was raised from a moral obligation to a legal duty. This legal force ensured the initial arrangements for the help of the poor and protection and support of Islam.

The legal quantum of Zakat is briefly stated below:

1. On agriculture produce of the irrigated lands 5% and non-irrigated lands 10%

2. On jewellery, merchandise and cash 10%

3. On animal pastured on public lands 1½% to 2½%.

4. On minerals and earth deposits 20%.

For every well-to-do Muslim it is a legal tariff. It cannot be reduced because this is the initial and inevitable limit of Zakat. If it goes by default, this pillar of the Faith will remain incomplete and the edifice of Islam would not be raised. Any reduction in this limit is out of question because what the prescribed rate of Zakat yields is insufficient for the objectives set forth for it. These objectives warrant that a Muslim should not be content with stipulated rate of Zakat only. He should pay much more than that. This voluntary payment should be a permanent feature so that there is a maximum possibility for the materialisation of these objectives. Although payment in excess of the prescribed rate is a discretionary matter yet it would be wrong to presume that after making this payment one has fully acquitted himself of his legal obligations. As far as the first category of objectives is concerned one may be free of his lability when he has paid the prescribed rate of Zakat. The Islamic law may not, make any further claim from him on this behalf. But this would not be the position in regard to the other two categories of objectives. He will still be bound to both of them. The Prophet s.a.w. once said:

"In the wealth of a Muslim his other religious fellows have a share over and above Zakat" (Tirmidhi).

It means that a Muslim is not free of his fiscal responsibilities even after the payment of the prescribed Zakat. There may still be a claim on him. This claim can be of three kinds, such as the claim of the soul for its purification, the claim of the poor for their help; the claim of the religion for its support and protection. These claims will be justified because the love of wealth may still persist in the heart of an individual. Hunger and starvation may still plague a society and the religion may still be in need of support and protection. As far as the purification of the heart is concerned it cannot be attained even if one gives his entire wealth away under legal pressure. It can come about only through voluntary spending. Compulsion and force would achieve nothing. Since the objectives of the other two categories can be achieved by means of law, they acquire the character of legal rights also. It leads us to the inference that if a Muslim Society fails to make an adequate arrangement for the protection and support of

Islam, this moral obligation is transformed into legal obligation. In the light of the above mentioned saying of the Prophet *s.a.w.* an Islamic state will be competent, rather liable, to levy a tax over and above Zakat on the affluent class of the society. This arrangement will provide the funds required for the needs of the poor and for the protection and support of Islam.

It seems pertinent to add here that in Islam the concept of a rich man is different from its usual sense. A Muslim, who, at the end of a year, possesses wealth in cash or kind equivalent to 52½ tolas of silver, is to be counted as a rich man in this context.

MANAGEMENT OF ZAKAT

Islam has given definite injunctions as to how Zakat should be collected and sent. Except Zakat one is free to give all alms as one likes. This freedom is not allowed in the case of Zakat. In this respect it is to some extent similar to the prayer which is performed in congregation. It has likewise a collective system. An Islamic state collects Zakat through its revenue and distributes it among the deserving people. No one can refuse to pay it to the government. The Qur'an prescribes its beneficiaries and specifies the heads of its expenditure. It also makes a special mention of those who work for the collection of Zakat. This specification of the Qur'an goes to prove that the collection and distribution of Zakat by the government is a religious obligation of the state and an accepted feature of the Islamic system. The practice in vogue in the times of the Prophet *s.a.w.* and his well-directed caliphs (Allah be pleased with them all) corroborates this view point. During the reign of the Caliph Abu Bakr (Allah be pleased with him) some people refused to pay Zakat to the government and he fought against them. He declared:

> "By Allah, if they withhold from me even the tether of a camel which they used to render to the Prophet *s.a.w.*, I would fight against them for it" *(Muslim)*.

The words "withhold from me" make it clear that Zakat is to be given to the government. The words "fight them for it" reveal that the disobedience against of this order amounts to revolt-an act which will be of no help, neither here nor in the Hereafter.

Such incidents took place in the reign of other well-directed caliphs also. Some of the tribes were exempted from this order. They were permitted to distribute Zakat collected by them among the poor-folk of their own areas. It is remarkable that they were exempted by the government and did not do so on their own. This departure from the rule was nothing but an official device necessitated by administrative expediency.

Such a system is necessary because of the following:

It is in accordance with the genius of Islam, which happens to be collectivise in character. What Islam wants to impart to the world can be attained only through its collective system. It enjoins the Muslims to live as a well-organised and disciplined society and to form a social order dominated by a maximum degree of discipline and collaboration.

Second: It was necessitated by considerations such as the welfare of the poor, extensive needs of the religion and the defence of Islam. One important thing, that could not be overlooked was the slackness of the rich in regard to their duty to the poor and the religion. In order to meet such a situation, and also to ensure that these rights were fully Protected, the responsibility of its collection was reposed in the Government.

If the exigencies of the collective system of Zakat are kept in view they will provide an answer to the question as to what would be the course for the payment of Zakat in states where the institution of Islamic Government does not exist. The establishment of prayer, especially the weekly and bi-annual prayers (Prayers of Friday and *Eids*) demands that it should be led by the caliph or his assistant. But it does not imply that in his absence each Muslim should say his

prayers separately. The alternative provided in such a situation is that
the Muslims of each locality should form an organisation of their
own and appoint one of them to lead their prayers. Similar is the case
of Zakat. It does not really matter if the institution of an Islamic
Government does not exist for the collection of Zakat. The cardinal
principles of Islam and its over-all conduct provide an alternate
course in such a situation. As Muslim communities join hands to
build their mosques, gather in them and pick a man to lead their
prayers, they should in the same manner arrange for the collection
and disbursement of their Zakat. The Muslims are enjoined to
establish a Public Treasury (*Bait-ul-Mal*) for this purpose. This
agency should be entrusted with the task of collection and distribution
of Zakat. In the absence of a state agency, such an institution would
ensure the fulfilment of the objectives of Zakat to the maximum
possible extent. If this arrangement is not made the entire Muslim
community of that locality will be at fault.

Variety of Terms used for Zakat

In the religious terminology of Islam two more terms also occur
for Zakat. They are alms (*Sadaqa*) and spending in the name of Allah
(*Infaq Fi Sabilillah*). The literal meanings of Zakat have already been
stated above. It would be relevant to discuss the meanings and
significance of the two terms, just mentioned. The term *Sadaqa*
comes from the word (*Sidq*) which means righteousness and sincerity
in the giver, but also proves that he has these virtues in him.
Similarly, *Infaq Fi Sabilillah* means spending in the service of Allah.
The ultimate objective of Zakat is to win Allah's pleasure. Zakat has
been called spending in the name of Allah as it is indicative of its
real spirit. Thus these three terms are not only three different names
of one and the same thing, they are also different aspects of the same
reality.

So far as the Qur'an is concerned it uses all the three words in
the same sense and connotation. Whatever is spent to please Allah is
Zakat,(poor-due) *Sadaqa* (almsgiving) and *Infaq Fi Sabilillah*

(expenditure in the service of Allah) at the same time. It is immaterial whether this expenditure relates to the legal tax (*Zakat*) or voluntary alms. None, of the words is meant to denote specific meaning of legal or voluntary alms and can be used alternately. It is for obvious reasons that the attention of the Qur'an and Tradition is focused on the real objective and purpose and not on the legal aspects of the matter they are dealing with. In Islamic jurisprudence Zakat is the expenditure which is legal and compulsory while the terms almsgiving (*Sadaqa*) and spending in the service of Allah (*Infaq Fi Sabilillah*) are used exclusively for voluntary alms. As jurisprudence is another name for law such differentiation of the terms was but necessary for its own purpose. The case of the Qur'an and the Tradition is very much different from jurisprudence and they have considered any discrimination in these terms unnecessary.

9

FASTING (Ṣaum)

The fourth pillar of Islam is "fasting". The technical term for it is
Ṣaum or *Ṣayam* which literally means to be at rest. It has been so
named for the reason that while one is keeping fast he abstains from
eating, drinking and sexual intercourse from dawn to dusk.

Special Significance and Features of the Fast

The injunctions in regard to the fast given in the Qur'an reveals that
it has numerous advantages and blessings. Some of these are of
fundamental importance. In order to understand the importance of the
fast it is essential to understand its following redeeming features.

Fast: A Source of Piety

The frst and foremost quality of the fast is that it creates piety and
fear of Allah. The Qur'an, the Tradition and the human reason
provide ample evidence to this effect. This fact has been explicitly
stated in the Qur'an where it makes fasting obligatory.

> *O ye who believe, fasting is prescribed for you, even as it was
> prescribed for those before you, that ye may ward off evil*
> (2:183).

A saying of the Prophet *s.a.w.* signifies the same thing in the
following words:

> "Fasting is a shield for you (as it saves you from sins in this
> world and would protect you from hell in the Hereafter)"
> (*Muslim*).

"Fasting is a shield against sins" is a reaffirmation of the fact that fasting makes a man pious. It is further added that:

"When any one of you is observing the fast, he should neither use indecent language nor speak aloud. If someone kicks up a row and abuses him, he should tell him that he is observing fast" (*Muslim*).

It means that although a Muslim has always to shun abusing and altercation, it becomes all the more essential when he is keeping fast. If he is not immune from these things in everyday life, he should at least avoid them during the fast. This saying of the Prophet *s.a.w.* is in fact a declaration that fasting is an accepted means of attaining piety and fear of Allah. It is an accepted means of piety and in one aspect or the other has a singular significance.

On this point the evidence of the Qur'anic verse is more than sufficient. There is no need to advance any argument in support of this contention. But for the purpose of greater satisfaction it would not be inappropriate if this fact is also verified by reason. Let us consider as to how and why fasting creates piety and fear of Allah in man.

First of all let us see what piety (*Taqwa*) really is. After knowing its precise meanings we will be in a position to understand as to how it is inculcated by fasting. Piousness (*Taqwa*) is the name of that profound care for saving ourselves from the displeasure of Allah which urges one for virtue and dissuades him from vice. In other words it is actually a state of mind which forms a practical attitude that helps attain the obedience and pleasure of Allah. One who is obsessed with such a feeling thinks all the time of nothing except the pleasure of Allah. He is always afraid lest he should do some thing which would displease Him. He is always worried lest he should miss anything which would please Him.

How this desire and effort of attaining the pleasure and escaping the displeasure of Allah is achieved. It can only be achieved if one has full control of himself and does not go by his whims. It means that the only way of attaining piety is that one does not leave his self unbridled and his desires unrestrained. It is clear from the following verse of the Qur'an:

> *But as for him who feared to stand before his Lord and restrained his soul from lust, Lo the Garden will be, his home* (70:40-41).

Now let us see what really the fast is? Three things are pre-requisite for the fast i.e. one should not eat, drink and copulate from dawn to dusk. In other words, one should totally abstain from the three demands of the self. These three things occupy vital place in the collective demand of the self. No other demand of the self is as important, as all-pervading and as forceful as these. On the one hand, these demands are so, pressing that one is subdued by them. On the other hand, they are not merely desires but instinctive urges of man also. Not only man's own existence but also his progeny depends on them. He is always in need of eating and drinking to keep himself alive and needs sexual contact for progeniture.

This latter position of these demands makes them doubly forceful. Their resistance becomes still more difficult on that account. The fast imposes the strongest check on these forceful demands. For full one month one keeps them at bay for twelve to fourteen hours a day. One feels such an acute thirst that he can hardly speak properly. He finds cold water at hand to slake his thirst. He feels an urge to drink but the fast deters him and he becomes helpless. Similar is the case of the other the desires. Imagine what power of restraint and contentment this exercise of thirty days will create in him. If one can keep under his control such strong instinctive urges for a considerable length of time, it should not be expecting too much of him that he would be able to subdue his other desires even more conveniently. It is a fact which cannot be denied. The admission of this fact really means that the fast creates in one full power of controlling his self and the urges emanating from it. It is a power with which he can easily beat down mischievous behaviour by his own self or of the Satan, in his adherence to the path of religion and Divine injunctions. In short, it makes him pious and fearful of Allah in the true sense.

There is also another factor which makes the fast a strong source of piety. The Prophet *s.a.w.* has referred to it in the following words:

"Fast is free from hypocrisy" (*Fathul Bari*).

The absence of the element of hypocrisy in a prayer is a guarantee of the fact that it brings a man near Allah. There can be no better and reliable source of piety than prayer. It would not be wrong to regard it as the richest food for piety. What doubt could there be in its being an effective means of piety when the Prophet *s.a.w.* has declared it as a permanent quality of the fast that it is free from hypocrisy? If prayers, which are not altogether immune from hypocrisy, can enrich one with the wealth of piety, such devotions which are absolutely free from it would definitely do more.

There is no secret about the fact that the fast is immune from hypocrisy. It is a kind of prayer which happens to be negative in character as it does not come into effect by doing certain acts (as in the case of prayer, poor-due and pilgrimage). Unlike other prayers it comes into effect by not doing certain acts. Obviously such a prayer can neither be seen nor heard by any one. A prayer which can neither be seen nor heard can have no chance of ostentation of hypocrisy. Thus among all the articles of faith the fast alone has this distinction that the devil of hypocrisy cannot attack it.

Apparently it was because of this distinctive position that the Qur'an used the words: *They may ward off (evil)* (2:183) for the fast alone. Injunctions in regard to no other prayer contain these words although it is an established fact that every prayer creates virtue and piety. It is also because of this distinguished position of the fast that Allah has regarded it as "His" or "for Him" and for the purpose of reward and remuneration regarded it as the weightiest of all.

"Every good act that a man does shall receive from ten to seven hundred rewards" says Allah "but the fast is an exception because it is for "Me" alone and I will give its rewards as much as I like. He who fasts abandons the lust and cravings of his appetite for My sake" (*Muslim*).

"Fast is for Me" signifies the fact that there is no hypocrisy in the fast.

If the purpose of the fast is to create piety and virtue in man than piousness is the real touchstone of fasting. If fasting lies in the abstinence from eating, drinking and sexual intercourse hen it means that one should be away from all such things which displease Allah. If a person not only controls these cravings but also subjects all his passions to the Divine injunctions he keeps the fast in the true sense. Otherwise his fast is but starvation. Fasting is not abstinence from food and sexual contact. This abstinence is only a mark and technical form of the fast. If someone is content with its apparent and physical form alone he is akin to one who goes round the domain of the fast and does not enter it. The Prophet *s.a.w.* has said:

"How many fasters there are for whom hunger and thirst are the result of their fast" (*Darimi*).

What kind of persons are they is explained in another saying of the Prophet *s.a.w.*:

"If a person does not abstain from telling lies or doing wrong when he is observing fast, let it be known to him that Allah does not want that he should stop eating his food" (*Bukhari*).

These sayings have made it clear that the real purpose of imposing restraint over the three appetites of man was to control his self through this exercise and training and if his nefarious activities continue even when he is observing the fast, it proves that he has either failed to grasp the real objective of the fast or he is no better than the one who does not observe it. As a matter of fact there is no difference between the person who does not keep fast and the one who keeps it without fulfilling its real purpose.

Fast : An Essential Means of Acquiring a Life of Piety

The second great importance of the fast lies in the fact that it is indispensable for acquiring the required standard of piety. Fast does not pave the way for piety but nevertheless it cannot be attained without it. There are other virtues and good deeds which foster piousness but the fast surpasses them all. No other act can serve as a substitute for fast.

This fact is revealed by the Qur'anic verse:

Even as it was prescribed for those before you (2:183).

If this verse was meant to convey that the fast has been prescribed for the Muslims so as to create in them the qualities of the pious life, then there was no need for the addition of these words. Because then the purpose of the addition of these words would have been the statement of a historical fact only, while it is an established fact that the Qur'an is far above the recording of historical facts as such. It does not say even a single word unless it has a religious significance. This religious significance can be no other than the one that the importance of fasting for a pious life may be fully emphasised. The Muslims were made aware of the real objective of fasting as well as the reason for its prescription in Islam. It was also to emphasise upon them that for attaining the required standard of piety fasting was of superb importance. For this purpose no other act could replace fasting. If it were not so the fast would not have been a pillar of faith in every Divine religion. Its prescription proves that, like prayer and poor-due, the fast has a natural affinity with the Divine religion. In the absence of the fast its disciplinary system of prayer would not be complete.

As regards the question as to why the fast is necessary for acquiring the essence of piety, it would be useful to reconsider the discussion already made which highlights the point how the fast creates piety in its observer? It is an established fact that the fasting is a very brief and effective exercise for creating self-discipline in man. It is also an admitted fact that the fast is a kind of prayer which does not include any element of hypocrisy. These two facts combined are sufficient to convince us of its importance for piety. If not fully, to a great extent at least, they explain the reason why fasting is so indispensable for an ordinary man. The other questions in this regard will be answered in the discussion that follows:

Fast: The Index of the Islamic Concept of Piety

The third importance of the fast is that in many respects it is the exponent of the real spirit of Islam. The concept of religion given in the Qur'an is reflected in the fast with all its important details. It means that the fast does not make a man pious in deeds but in thought and outlook also. It imparts piousness and spells out its full significance. This point is elucidated by the following saying of the Prophet s.a.w.:

1. "He who goes on fasting all his life, his fast becomes void" (*Bukhari*).

2. "You should strictly refrain from the fast extending continuously over two or more days" (*Muslim*).

3. In the course of a journey the Prophet s.a.w. saw a crowd of men gathered round a person. Inquiry revealed that a traveller was keeping fast and men had collected about him. The Prophet s.a.w. said:

    "It is no good to keep fast during a journey, the hardship of which is beyond the strength of an ordinary man" (*Bukhari*).

4. A companion of the Prophet s.a.w., who lived somewhere outside Medina came to the Prophet s.a.w. and went back after meeting him. After a year he came again. On this visit he was

much reduced in health. He felt that he has not been recognised. He asked the Prophet s.a.w. if he had recognised him. The Prophet s.a.w. replied that he did not. The visitor said that the was the same person who had come last year. The Prophet s.a.w. asked what had happened to him because last year he looked bright and healthy. He replied that ever since his visit last year he had taken his food once a day only (he had been keeping fast). When the Prophet s.a.w. heard of it he said: Why did you torture yourself? (*Abu Dawud*)

If we consider the far-reaching implications of these traditions we will discover that the fast enunciates a revolutionary concept of piety. These traditions emphasise that the piety, which is the main objective of the fast, is not self-effacement. It is self-control. In other words it does not foster piety alone. It also reveals those of its secrets as are very little known and understood. When we hear of the fast, what immediately comes to our mind is the perpetual denial of the demands of the self. He who denies more of them is held in higher esteem in the realm of piety. The Qur'an says:

But as for him who feared to stand before his Lord and restrained his soul from lust (79:40).

The fear of Allah (piety) is not attained if the self is restrained from its passions. But the important of the above mentioned sayings of the Prophet s.a.w. and the fast itself, signify that this is certainly not the meaning of this verse of the Qur'an. The true significance of the fast in Islam is quite different. What it expects of man and what it really means by *Bir* (virtue) and *Taqwa* (fear of Allah) is only this that man should not let his 'self' go unrestrained. He must check his 'self' from following its whims and subject it to the Divine injunctions. It does not mean that he should mortify his 'self' with perpetual tortures and kill its instinctive urges. In the opinion of others it may be a very high and noble purpose, but in Islam it is something reprehensible. It is neither a correct mode of devotion nor is consonant with the true spirit of Islam. Judged by the Islamic standards it is not virtue but its opposite. The existence of the fast is a constant reminder of this reality. Some other sayings of the Prophet *s.a.w.* relevant to this subject are given below:

1. "Do take the meals at dawn before starting the fast. It has a great blessing" (*Muslim*).

2. "As long as people will hasten in the breaking of the fast (at the stipulated time) they will be in a state of goodness" (*Muslim*).

3. "Divine religion shall dominate as long as people will make haste in breaking their fasts (at the stipulated time)" (*Abu Dawud*).

4. "Allah says that My most beloved person is one who hastens to break fast (at the stipulated time)" (*Tirmidhi*)

The vital and revolutionary fact disclosed by the traditions quoted earlier is further highlighted by the latter traditions, and make this concept perfect. The traditions quoted earlier revealed that piety did not mean self-effacement but self-control. The latter traditions explain that this self-control includes 'discipline of views' and 'discipline of liking' also. In other words as 'self' is made subject to the Divine injunctions, similarly in the practice of the Divine injunctions one should not exercise his personal liking and opinion. The true piety is not attained merely by withholding the self from the violation of the Divine injunctions. It is imperative that in their compliance, as in search for the pleasure of Allah, one must not let his own opinion, predilection and liking to count even if they appear to be subscribing to piousness. Man should worship Allah, both in the negation of associates ascribed to Him and affirmation of His Oneness, exactly in the manner he is ordained. As he kills those passions which obstruct compliance of the Divine injunctions, similarly he should not pay any heed to his own views in matters relating to the dimensions of the Divine injunctions. For him submission to Allah and a life of piety should constitute what Allah and His Prophet *s.a.w.* have ordained. He should comply with, and abstain from, things exactly within the framework of Divine injunctions. He should so behave that his heart is satisfied with the belief that he has complied with the Divine injunctions precisely as they are prescribed. As a certain act of religion is compliance of a Divine injunction, and its performance is piousness and submission to Allah, so is the fact that in his submission he should confine himself strictly to the boundaries of the Divine injunctions. He must strictly abstain from adding anything of his own.

The self control which the fast inculcates, includes in its scope the 'discipline of views' and 'the discipline of liking'. This statement hardly needs any elaboration. It will be observed that on the one hand these traditions hold that the object of the fast is to foster piety. On the other hand, they give a stern warning to those who observe the fast without taking the meals preceding it. Such a person deprives himself of a great blessing. Similar is the position of the breaking of the fast. Delay in breaking the fast is held as a mark of decline of virtue and faith.

When these two things are put together it will become clear that keeping of the fast, without taking the meals preceding it, and delay in breaking the fast are contrary to the object of piety. Although both these things would have proved helpful in the subjection of the self. They also seem to be in line with the efforts necessary for attaining the purpose of the fast. But the Prophet *s.a.w.* says that the factual position is quite contrary. Why is it so? One possible answer to this question is that the absence of these two restrictions would have cleared the way for interference. Because of personal opinions and likes and dislikes of individuals the prescribed things of the fast would not have been observed properly. The prescribed time of the fast is of vital importance and any extension in its duration is contrived for selfish motives. In fact it amounts to projecting one's own opinion and liking in the matter of religion. If it is so, then it will be admitted that the fast does not aim at 'self-control' only but also puts a restrain over one's opinion and liking in matters of religion. The interpretation of the concept of piety which the fast gives is comprehensive. It makes the freedom of opinion and liking as much subject to the Divine injunctions as it does the freedom of passions.[1]

If we glance at the redeeming features of the fast, it will not be difficult to know why it has been regarded as a pillar of Islam and why the edifice of Islam cannot be completed without it.

---

[1] This concept of piety and the above mentioned sayings of the Prophet *s.a.w.* may seem strange to an ordinary man. But this very strangeness is in fact a special trait of the true religions. The fact is, that it was in view of the understanding of the ordinary men that the Prophet *s.a.w.* elucidated such things. He *s.a.w.* had before him the history of earlier nations, instances of the distortion of other religions and the philosophies of self-mortification and asceticism. He (peace be upon him) knew that the Divine religion was not destroyed by the worshippers of the 'self' but adulterate by the exaggeration and inflated zeal of the pious. One thing that was not effected by this element was fast. It was turned into a prolonged spell of starvation on the naive presumption that the longer the fast, the greater would be the attainment of its objectives. This concept went so far that self-mortification and asceticism became the height of religiosity. This was the background in which the Prophet *s.a.w.*, in his capacity being Allah's final Messenger, considered it apt to warn people and take all measures to protect Islam from the dangers the earlier Divine religions had to face and which were ultimately responsible for their distortion. He took special care to protect the fast from becoming a refuge of the practices like self-mortification, abstention from pleasure and asceticism. He made it absolutely clear that the duration of the fast prescribed by Allah was to be observed meticulously. If this restriction is not observed its results would be disastrous one would be labouring under the impression that he is acting in accordance with the injunctions of Allah and he would benefit from it, while the actual position would be quite different. Apparently it may be an act of piety and submission to Allah, and something intended for the pleasure of Allah alone, but as it will not be in conformity with the real spirit of Islam, it will demolish the real concept of its prayer. This would result in a loss impossible to repair. If the flag-bearers of the Divine religion wore ignorant of their precise aim, how would they perform their duty properly. If this vital afgnificance is kept in view it will bring home the importance of beginning and breaking the fast at stipulated times, which otherwise appears an insignificant issue. In fact it is a problem of maintaining the true concept of religion. Adherence to the times prescribed for the beginning and closing of the fast is as a matter of fact an indispensable endeavour for protecting the true spirit of religion. Disregard of these limits would eventually lead to distortion in religious matters. If the true concept of religion is tinged with streak of ascetisim it will not leave any chance of keeping the Islamic society in a state of holiness. It will not help the religion to maintain dominant position.

Some Special Blessings of the Fast

After knowing that the fast invests a man with piety, nothing important remains to be discussed on this premise because one who
attains piety would do what Allah and His Prophet s.a.w. enjoin upon
him. This is something which covers all the requirements of religion.
Still there are certain benefits which the fast yields as its special
blessings. It would greatly help us in understanding the vital
significance of the fast if we cast a glance over them also.

1. The fast strengthens one's faith in the sovereignty of Allah. It is
    dawn and time for the meals preceding the fast. One is free to
    eat. Then comes the white line on the horizon and with its
    appearance one withdraws himself from food. This abstinence
    from food and other pleasures of life, despite their accessibility,
    will now continue till evening. As the sun sets the fast comes to
    an end. One must eat something to break it. This entire system
    of order and compliance is such a manifestation of authority and
    obedience which one does not find in any other act of religion.
    This phenomenon makes the supremacy of Allah akin to an eye
    witness account.

2. Fasting creates a wave of sympathy and fellow-feeling in an
    Islamic Society. The rich are made to experience the pangs of
    poverty for one month continuously. At least for thirty days it
    reminds them of the hardships of starvation and hunger. This
    practical experience and feeling creates in them a determination
    for the amelioration of the poor. In this way fasting develops in
    them the spirit of sympathy and spending in the way of Allah.
    For this reason the Prophet s.a.w. has regarded the month of
    fasting as "the month of sympathy". It was the practice of the
    Prophet s.a.w. that during the month of the fast (Ramadan) he
    used to set all his slaves free. Nor did he ever deny a beggar's
    request.

    "When it was the month of Ramadan he (the Holy Prophet)

emancipated every slave and gave charity to every one who asked for it" (*Mishkat*).

According to the statement of Ibn Abbas although the Prophet *s.a.w.* was the most generous of men, yet in the month of the fast his generosity became extraordinary.

Allah's Apostle *s.a.w.* was the most generous among mankind and he was (particularly) most gracious in the month of Ramadan (*Bukhari*).

3. Fasting strengthens the sense of equality. During the month of the fast all members of the Muslim Society, the rich and the poor, the ruler and the ruled, the elite and the ordinary, are in a similar position. All share an equal level of obedience.

Their faces reflect that they are slaves of one Master and subject to Him in equal degree. This state of mind purges them of all their notions of rank and status and gives a complexion of equality to the whole Muslim Society.

4. Fast prepares its observer for struggle in the cause of Allah. For this one has to endure the hardships of hunger, thirst and other discomforts one suffers all this for the pleasure of Allah. One spends his wealth and even lays down his life for it. Such a feat can only be ventured by one who has the strength of endurance. He alone can go through these ordeals who has the power to persevere. Fasting is the best training for it. It is the best way of getting accustomed to hardships. For this reason the Prophet s.a.w. regarded this month (Ramadan) as "the month of patience" and called the fast as "half patience".

5. The method laid down for the prescribed fast intensifies the feeling of national unity. It constantly reminds them of their being the flag bearers of one mission. The injunctions regarding the fast require that every one should observe the fast in the prescribed month (Ramadan). One who observes the fast should

take his meals little before dawn and break his fast at sun-set immediately. The institution of the fast is so planned that the Muslims observe fast at the same time. What an ideal arrangement it is for infusing the members of a community with the spirit that they are working for the same mission and engaged in the same campaign that even their food is subject to a uniform order and discipline.

Conditions for the Attainment of the Objectives of the Fast

Like every other act of worship the objectives of the fast can only be attained if:

1. It is observed with all its requisite formalities and conditions. Sincerity of purpose, fear of Allah and firm faith that Allah and Allah alone is to be worshipped and man is nothing but His humble bondsman, passion for submission to His pleasure and craving for the betterment in the Afterlife are some of the pre-requisites of the fast. In the words of the Prophet *s.a.w.* fast is observed with "faith and self-analysis". If the fast s bereft of the belief in the sovereignty of Allah and humbleness of man and hope for reward in the Afterlife, the fast is reduced to bare starvation. In such a situation he who is keeping the fast would be under the impression that he is doing his duty and constr-ucting a pillar of the faith while actually there would be no such thing worth its name even.

2. One must not rest contented with the obligatory fasts only. He should also observe the non-obligatory fasts also. By these fasts he will be constantly reminded of the objectives for which the fast has been prescribed. Thereby he will also be repeating the practical exercise of the training of the self in months other than the one prescribed for fasting. Complete detail as to the number of nonobligatory fasts and when they are to be observed is given in the traditions. Each individual can choose from them such fasts as suits his capacity and circumstances.

10

THE PILGRIMAGE (Ḥajj)

The fifth and the last pillar of Islam is Pilgrimage. Literally it means to make up one's mind to visit a Holy place. Technically this mode of worship is called Pilgrimage (*Hajj*) because in it one intends to set out for Ka'bah.

The Importance of Pilgrimage

Every Muslim is duty-bound to perform the pilgrimage once in his life-time, if he is an adult and has the means to undertake a journey to Mecca. If any one who despite his means does not go for the pilgrimage he belies his own claim of being a Muslim. The Qur'an says:

> *And pilgrimage to the House is a duty unto Allah for mankind, for him who can find a way thither. As for him who disbelieveth (let him know that) Lo! Allah is independent of all creatures* (3: 97).

"One who is not held back by some genuine problem or by a tyrant ruler and still does not go on the pilgrimage, it makes little difference whether he dies a Jew or a Christian" (*Sunan -e -Kubra*).

Umar, the Great (*r.a.*) is said to have stated:

"He should die as a Jew or a Christian (he repeated these words three times) who in spite of having the means to travel and a peaceful passage dies without performing the pilgrimage" (*Sunan-e-Kubra*).

As opposed to this, one who properly performs this sacred rite has been commanded so highly that nothing better can be wished for.

"Nothing but the Heaven is the reward of an approved pilgrimage" (*Muslim*).

"One who goes on the pilgrimage of the House of Allah and in the course of the pilgrimage neither commits any sensual act nor any other sin he returns as innocent as a new born baby" (*Bukhari*).

Why have Allah and His Prophet *s.a.w.* attached importance of the highest degree to the pilgrimage, why in its absence the claim of being a Muslim is worthless and how does it guarantee a safe passage to Paradise? In order to find out the answers to these questions we shall have to see what the pilgrimage really is? What has it got to do with the spirit of religion? What part does it play in forming an intellect and a character which is Islamic in outlook? How does it help a Muslim in the performance of his duty of Allah's worship, which is the sole purpose of his creation? We can learn all this from two things: First, What is the Ka'bah where people go on their pilgrimage? What was it built for? What connection has it with Islam? Secondly, what rites are performed in the pilgrimage and what concepts are at work in these rites?

If all these points are studied in detail they will explain why the pilgrimage has been given the importance of the highest degree.

The Construction of Ka'bah and its Significance

First of all, it us see the history of the construction of Ka'bah and its significance. It was constructed about four and a half thousand years ago by Ibrahim (*a.s.*) and his son Isma'il (*a.s.*).

And when Ibrahim and Isma'il were raising the foundations of the House (2:127).

Both the construction of Ka'bah and the selection of its site were decreed by Allah.

And (remember) when We prepared for Ibrahim the place of the Holy House (22:26).

When its construction was completed they were ordered to proclaim that a pilgrimage unto it was a duty.

And proclaim unto mankind the pilgrimage (22:27).

The purpose and significance attached to this House by Allah are made clear in the following verse of the Qur'an:

And when We made the House (at Mecca) a resort for mankind and a sanctuary (saying): Take as your place of worship the place where Ibrahim stood (to pray) (2:125).

Lo! the first sanctuary appointed for mankind was that at Becca (Mecca), a blessed place a guidance to the people (3:96).

And (remember) when We prepared for Ibrahim the place of the (Holy) House, saying: Ascribe thou nothing as partner unto Me, and purify My House for those who stand and those who bow and make prostration" (22:26).

It means that this House is an embodiment of goodness and blessing. It is a fountain-head of guidance, a place of worship for the pious and a place the prayer is directed towards and a centre of the Unity of Allah. A careful study would reveal that these merits have a close affinity with each other. It would be more true to say that these are the various facets of a comprehensive merit. A place which is the centre of the pure unity, must be a place the prayers are directed to. Logically a place which is the centre of the true unity should also be the lighthouse of guidance and goodness.

In the discussions already made in this book we have seen that in faith, the Unity of Allah, and in practise the stipulated prayer constitute the essence of religion. If the Ka'bah is a point where the

Unity and the prayer converge then it would be right to say that it is the centre of the entire religion. For this reason it has been regarded by Allah as His own House". It clearly means that Ka'bah is the house or the centre of the Divine religion.

How did this sacred House built by Ibrahim (*a.s.*) become the abode of Divine religion and the centre of Islam? In order to understand this question we must know the background of its construction. It is also important to know that when its construction was completed what practical steps were taken to attain the objectives which led to its construction.

Following is the background of its construction:

When Ibrahim (peace by upon him) was forced by his people to migrate he abandoned his house and set out for religious preaching and inviting people towards righteousness. After visiting a number of places he at last arrived in the barren valley of Mecca. It was here that the famous incident of Ibrahim's dream occurred. He dreamt that he was sacrificing his son (Isma'il) with his own hands. When he mentioned this dream to Isma'il (*a.s.*.)he immediately conceded that Allah's command must be obeyed. He assured his father that he would undergo the sacrifice with patience and obeisance. Ibrahim (*a.s.*.)laid down his son on the ground and placed the knife across his throat. When he was about to perform the sacrifice he heard a voice saying: Ibrahim hold your hands. You have verified the vision. We have ransomed Isma'il. A big sacrifice shall be his ransom. (37:103-107)

The whole life of Ibrahim (*a.s.*.)was full of trials. This incident of the sacrifice was the last in the sequence. His success in this ordeal opened a vista of Divine reward for him. He was given a good tiding from Allah:

I have appointed thee a leader for mankind (2:124).

This ceremony of installing Ibrahim (*a.s.*.)as a leader of mankind started with the Divine orders for the erection of Ka'bah and proclamation and injunctions referred above.

Two redeeming features of this incident are to be kept specially in mind:

1. The incident of the sacrifice occurred at Mina, a place situated close to Mecca.

2. The determination which Ibrahim and Isma'il (peace be upon them) showed for turning the vision into an accomplished fact is designated by Allah as "Islam" which means (surrender or submission).

    Then, when they had surrendered (to Allah) and had flung him (Isma'il) down upon his face (37:103).

In order to achieve the objectives of its construction through following steps were taken:

When the construction was started its venerable builders prayed to Allah for the fulfilment of its objectives in the following words:

And when Ibrahim and Isma'il were raising the foundations of the House (both of them supplicated): Our Lord, accept from us; surely Thou art All-Hearing and All-Knowing. Our Lord ! and make us submissive unto Thee, and of our progeny a nation submissive unto Thee, and show us our ways of worship, and relent towards us. Thou art the Relenting, the Merciful (2:127-128).

This prayer shows that the purpose for which Ka'bah was being built will be completed by the progeny of its builders.

This point needs special attention that in his prayer which asks that the venerable group be blessed with certain qualities, the word used is "Muslim" which means "One who submits".

When the construction of Ka'bah was completed Ibrahim

(*a.s.*.)did not take his son and wife to some other place. He settled down with them in that barren plain near Ka'bah so that the "group submissive unto Thee" would be born near it. Ibrahim (*a.s.*.)himself prayed:

> *Our Lord! Lo! I have settled some of my posterity in the uncultivable valley near the Holy House, our Lord that they may establish proper worship* (14: 37).

"That they may establish proper worship" means that they may render service to Allah, follow and preach His religion. It has already been explained that the prayer is the essence of the faith and the establishing of prayer is nothing but the establishment of entire religion.

How would this obedient group "a nation submissive" emerge out of the posterity of Isma'il (peace be upon him)? How would it know the way of true submission to Allah? For this purpose they uttered the following prayer:

> *Our Lord! and raise up in their midst a Messenger from among them who shall recite unto them Thy revelations and shall teach them the Book and the wisdom and shall purify them...* (2:129).

It need hardly be mentioned that those were the two prayers which were blessed by Allah and ultimately materialised in the person of the Prophet Muhammad *s.a.w.* and his companions (may Allah be happy with them all). This venerable group was known as "Muslim" and "a nation submissive". It was so named because Ibrahim (*a.s.*.)had remembered them in his prayer with this word and name. In other words it was Ibrahim (*a.s.*.)who gave this name to them. This fact is also confirmed by *Surah* "Hajj" of the Qur'an.

These facts make it quite clear why Ka'bah is the centre and fountainhead of Islam.

Rites of the Pilgrimage

Let us now take up the rites and ceremonies that are performed during the pilgrimage.

When a Muslim sets out on the pilgrimage he makes a declaration of his intention at a specified stage near Mecca. In technical terms it is called "*Ihram*". Before entering into *Ihram*, and putting on the garment specified for the pilgrimage, he has to take a bath or perform ablution. After the bath he replaces his ordinary dress by the pilgrim's sacred robe. It consists of two seamless sheets. One is wrapped round the waist and the other thrown loosely over the shoulders. Then he performs two *rak'ah* prayers and makes a formal declaration of his intention of making the pilgrimage. He addresses Allah and recites aloud :

Labbaika! Allahumma! Labbaika! Labbaika! La Sharika Laka! Labbaika! Innal Hamda wan Ni'mata Laka, wal Mulka La Sharika Laka"!

(I stand up for Thy service, O Allah! I stand up! I stand up! There is no partner with Thee! I stand up! I stand up! Verily Thine is the Praise, the Blessing and the Kingdom! There is no partner with Thee!)

As soon as he says the words "*Labbaika*" (I stand up!) "*Labbaika*" (I stand up!) he enters into the state of *Ihram*. Hence forth he goes on repeating these words on every occasion.

After every prayer, on ascending every height and descending every slope, at awakening, on meeting a caravan, in short in all events these words are at his lips. After assuming the *Ihram* every article of decoration and comfort is forbidden to him. He has already put away his ordinary dress. So much so that even the two sheets of cloth that are covering his body are unstitched. He is not permitted to wear coloured sheets. He cannot cover his face. Nor can he wear any headgear. Nor is he allowed to cut his hair or pare his nails. Nor is he permitted to use perfumes. Even the use of soap while bathing is not permissible. Sexual contact is absolutely forbidden. Even its mention is prohibited. He is not allowed to hunt nor can he guide anyone to a hunting place. Thus he proceeds towards Mecca. When he catches a glimpse of Ka'bah he shouts with joy *Allah-o-Akbar! Allah-o-Akbar! La ilaha ill-Allah* (Allah is Great! Allah is Great! There is no god but Allah!). After entering Mecca he goes straight to Ka'bah. Near the gate of Ka'bah is placed a black stone (known as *Al-Hajarul Aswad*). He places both his hands at this sacred stone and kisses it. Then he makes seven circuits round Ka'bah. After that he performs two rak'ah prayers in *Maqam-i-Ibrahim* (the place of Ibrahim) or at any other place in Ka'bah. When he comes out of Ka'bah he climbs the mount Safa which is quite close to it. From there he casts a glance at Ka'bah and recites :

Allah-o-Akbar! (Allah is Great!)

La Ilaha ill-Allah (There is no god but Allah)

After that he recites benediction for the Prophet *s.a.w.* and prays to Allah. Then he descends from "Mount Safa" and runs towards another hill known by the name of "Marwah" and repeats the prayer which he performed at Mount Safa". He runs through it seven times. After that he stays at Mecca and makes circuits of Ka'bah (*tawaf*) according to his capacity. Upon the seventh day (of the month of the Pilgrimage) the pilgrims gather in the mosque of Ka'bah and listen to the sermon of their leader in which he mentions the injunctions, rites, significance and blessings of the pilgrimage. On the eighth day the pilgrims proceed to Mina which is at a distance of three miles from Mecca. They stay there till the next morning and then proceed towards Arafat which is a vast plain at a distance of twelve miles from Mecca. The pilgrims arrive there before the midday prayer. When the sun begins to decline at midday they again listen to an oration from their leader. After the oration he leads a prayer wherein he combines the two prayers or the noon (*Zuhr*) and afternoon (*Asr*). After the prayers the pilgrims camp there in such a manner that their leader settles near the mount "Rahmat". He remains seated on his camel and does not step down. With his face towards Ka'bah he prays ardently. In the course of his prayer he frequently repeats :

"I stand up for Thy service, O Allah I stand up!

The rest of the congregation stands behind him and follows this prayer. On this occasion their leader once again delivers an oration which the pilgrims listen with rapt attention. After the sunset the pilgrims go to a place known as "al-Muzdalifah" and occupy the seats allotted to them. Their leader stays near the "Mount Qazah". At sunset he leads a prayer in which he combines the two prescribed prayers of the evening and the night. Then the pilgrims stay here for the night. On the tenth day the morning prayer is performed at an early hour. After this prayer every pilgrim is engrossed in repenting begging Allah's pardon, seeking His benediction and in remembering Him. All along he keeps repeating:

I stand up for Thy service, O Allah! I stand up!

When daylight appears, the pilgrims set out for Mina. Here they perform the ritual of throwing pebbles at the three satanic pillars situated there. They strike each pillar with seven pebbles and each time recite *Allah-o-Akbar!* (Allah is Great!).

Henceforth the pilgrims do not repeat the slogan "I stand up! O Allah! I stand up!" When the ritual of casting the pebbles is over the pilgrims sacrifice some cattle (a sheep, or a goat, or a cow or a camel according to the means of a pilgrim). It is a stipulated act. After the sacrifice they get their heads shaved and come out of the state of Ihram. Once again they perform seven circuits of Ka'bah (*tawaf*) and thereafter proceed to Mina. They stay there for two or three days. During this stay they spend their time in the remembrance of Allah and pray to Him for their forgiveness. Once again they throw pebbles on the three satanic pillars at Mina. This ritual is combined with the repetition of the slogans "Allah is Great!" Then the pilgrims come back to Ka'bah and again make circuits round it. When this ritual is over they kiss the gate of Ka'bah and touch with their faces and chests the place called "*Multazam*" which lies between "the Black Stone" (*Al-Hajarul Aswad*) and the "Gate of Ka'bah" (*Bab-i-Ka'bah*). Holding the cover of Ka'bah they vehemently weep, beg and pray to Allah for their welfare. Thereafter they return to their homes in such a state of mind that their hearts are full of mixed emotions of love and grief —love for the House of Allah and grief for departing from that sacred place.

This is a brief account of the rites of the pilgrimage. Many points included in this account are quite clear. There are a few which have a particular background. Their significance can only be grasped if we understand their background as well. For this purpose the salient features of these points are given below

1.   *Ka'bah*

As far as Ka'bah is concerned vital information in regard to it has been given in the discussion above.

2.   *Safa and Marwah*

In regard to the mounts 'Safa' and 'Marwah' the Qur'an says:

Lo! (the mountains As-Safa and Al-Marwah are among the indications of Allah (2:158).

The words "among the indications of Allah" clearly denote submission to Allah. In order to discover why they are so, we shall have to go back to their history. It reveals that as-Safa and al-Marwah are the places where Hajirah, the mother of Isma'il, ran for the search of water and the fountain of Zam Zam gush forth near these hills.

3.   *Jamarit*

In the plain of Mina, at short intervals, there are three pillars, each known as Jamrah. On grammatical priniciples when they are mentioned collectively they are called "*Jamarat*".

These are the places where Satan tried to waver Hadrat Ibrahim (*a.s.*), when he was going to sacrifice his dear son Isma'il (*a.s.*) in the way of Allah at Mina.

The Pilgrimage and the Sentiments of Worship

If we go deep into the significance of the rites of the pilgrimage we will find each of them illustrative of man's submission to Allah.

1.   The sacred garment which a pilgrim puts on during pilgrimage
(known as *Ihram*) is not a dress. It is on the one hand a mark of
man's servitude and on the other a symbol of his sacrifice. When a
beggar stretches his begging bowl before a benevolent master, or a
soldier goes to a battlefield in full military equipment and uniform,
his aims and sentiments need no words. His appearance makes every
thing self-evident. Similarly the appearance of a pilgrim shows that
he is nothing but a beggar of Allah. He is indifferent to everything
except the Divine pleasure. He abandons all worldly pursuits and is
completely occupied with His thought. He is imbued with the spirit
to sacrifice himself on a Divine command. He is both a bondsman
and a devoted soldier of Allah.

The garment of the pilgrims, *Ihram,* makes another declaration
also. When pilgrims from all corners of the world put off their
ordinary dress and wear pilgrim's sacred robe and shout the same
slogan

"I stand up! O Allah! I stand up!"

the Islamic nation becomes a visible reality. Even the blind would
see that the relationship of Islam is stronger than any other link The
real bond that unites man with man is this relationship. When the
whole atmosphere resounds with the slogans:

"I stand up for Thy Service, O Allah! I stand up!"

It seems that these slogans wore in response to the proclamation
which the founder of Ka'bah had made in obedience to the Divine
Command:

And proclaim unto mankind the pilgrimage (22:27).

2.   The proclamation which Ibrahim (*a.s.*.)made was not for the
performance of some plain rituals only. It was meant for imbibing the
spirit of the Faith and the essence of Islam. This is why its response:
"I stand up for Thy service, O Allah! I stand up!" is not an empty
slogan. It is an expression of a craving to submit oneself to Allah. It

is a declaration that a humble servant is at the command of his Master and submits to Him.

3.   As a pilgrim looks at Ka'bah the whole panorama associated with its construction comes to his mind. It reminds him that he is member of a nation for whose creation Ibrahim (a.s..)had prayed to Allah and whom he had called a nation submissive". He had prayed for a nation that would devote itself to Allah and His religion.

4.   When a pilgrim places his hands on the Black Stone (Al-Hajarul Aswad) he feels as if he was giving his hands in the hands of Allah in order to renew his covenant of submission and servitude and to ratify his commitment. After placing his hands on "the Black Stone" he kisses it. This gesture awakens in him another consciousness. He is reminded of the fact that Allah, for whom he is refreshing his covenant, is his 'real' Sovereign and Master. He and He alone deserves his worship and love. It is, therefore, necessary that when he is present in His House he should kiss its threshold as a mark of his love for Allah.

5.   What is Tawaf (circuit round Ka'bah)? It is nothing, but the expression of an ardent passion for sacrificing oneself for the pleasure of Allah. When a Muslim makes circuits round Ka'bah he is imbued with the legendary fervour which the moth possesses for the candle. He becomes an embodiment of submission, a personification of love. He loses consciousness of himself and is always anxious to sacrifice himself on a Divine command. He craves to attain Him even at the cost of his life.

The ritual of making circuits round Ka'bah is an indication of something else as well. When a vast multitude of pilgrims coming from different countries and consisting of various races and colours makes the circuits with a unanimous appearance and spirit, it is a reaffirmation of the fact that as Allah is One and His religion is one, similarly all His true believers are one. Their apparent differences are but superficial. They have one focal point and one centre. Their obedience and sacrifices are devoted for Allah and Allah alone.

6.   The ritual of running between the mounts Safa and Marwah is an expression of the pilgrims resolution that they remember the struggle of the illustrious Lady Hajirah in the compliance of Allah's order and will ever be ready for it.

7.   From the seventh to the tenth day of the month of Hajj (last month of Islamic calendar in which the pilgrimage is performed) the pilgrims are led by one leader. They move and stop together. One day they are together at Masjid-i-Haram, on the next they assemble at the plain of Mina, the next morning finds them camped at Arafat, at night they stay in Muzdalifah and when day comes round they are back in Mina. Similarly during the ceremonies they at one time listen to the oration of their leader and at another shout the slogan: "I stand up for Thy service, O Allah! I stand up!" They are in a hurry to perform their stipulated prayer. In haste they sometimes combine the two prayers in one. All these activities present the spectacle of a disciplined military life. This vast multitude of pilgrims, dressed in sacred garment looks like a large army ready to lay down their lives for Allah. This aspect proves to the hilt that the idea of a well-disciplined collective life and a martial conduct is inseparable from the concept of "a nation submissive". All the energies of this nation are devoted for the service of Allah, victory of His cause and glorification of His religion.

8.   The ritual of casting pebbles at the three pillars at Mina marks the remembrance of that great event in which the army of Abraha was destroyed by stones flung upon them by flying birds. This ceremony which is accompanied by the recital: "*Allah O-Akbar*" is in fact a pilgrim's challenge to the world. It is an expression of their firm resolve that those who cast a malicious look on the Divine religion will be destroyed by them. It is a declaration of their determination that whoever attacks this sacred place will be completely crushed.

9.   *Eid-ul-Adha* is a festival in commemoration of the great sacrifice that Allah has regarded as ransom for Prophet Isma'il *(a.s.)*.

Then We ransomed with a tremendous victim (37:107).

The sacrifice of an animal in the path of Allah is in fact akin to sacrificing oneself. It is a quiet admission that our lives are devoted to Allah. Whenever they will be asked by Him to give their lives, they will do it immediately. The blood that flows of the sacrificed animal denotes that they also will readily out offer their blood whenever it will be so required by Allah. This sacrifice has no meaning and significance other than those stated above because otherwise mere slaughter of animals would neither be a religious act nor a good deed.

Their flesh and their blood reach not Allah, but the devotion from you reacheth Him (22:37).

A study of the rites of the pilgrimage to Mecca will reveal that there is hardly a form of submission that is not included in it. Particularly the spirit of warfare in the cause Allah which is height of submission, permeates all these enactments so thoroughly that the whole pilgrimage takes on, both practically and intellectually, the appearance of a massive symbolic exercise of warfare. This is the reason why when Hazrat 'Ayeshah (*radiallahu anha*) asked, "We see that Jihad is the first of action, why should not we women also participate in it and do our duty?" the Holy Prophet *s.a.w.* replied:

"For womankind the finest of action is to perform an immaculate pilgrimage" (*Bukhari*).

Comprehensive Character of the Pilgrimage

Beside the merits of the pilgrimage stated above, if we see it from a different angle pilgrimage appears but one mode of worship. In fact it includes every kind of worship and good deed. It is so because:

1. Pilgrimage constitutes prayer as prayer is nothing but the remembrance of Allah. It has already been observed that pilgrimage is full of the remembrance of Allah.

2. Pilgrimage is poor-due as it is obligatory for every pilgrim that he should feed the poor with the flesh of the animal he

sacrifices:

And feed therewith the poor unfortunate (22:28).

It is evident that the sole purpose of spending wealth on pilgrimage is the pleasure of Allah. In its absence the pilgrimage will be of little consequence. Similar is the significance of the *Zakat* (poor-due) which is spent for the pleasure of Allah.

3. Pilgrimage also includes elements of the fast. For instance, sexual contact is forbidden during the course of the fast at daytime. In the pilgrimage it is forbidden at night as well. It is true that during the pilgrimage there is no restriction on eating which is completely prohibited in fast, but abstention from every kind of finery and decoration takes its place in pilgrimage. The exercise of controlling the passions of the self is as much a part of the pilgrimage as it is of the fasting.

4. Pilgrimage also imparts faith in the Unity of Allah because Ka'bah was founded on this very concept. A look at Ka'bah strengthens the unitarian faith of a Muslim. Several rites of the pilgrimage i.e., repeated slogans of "I stand up for Thy service, O Allah! I stand up!" the kissing of "the Black Stone" (*Al-Hajarul Aswad*)", circuits round Ka'bah, running between the mounts of Safa and Marwah, sacrificing animals on the *Eid* festival (tenth day of the month of the Pilgrimage) and other rites of the pilgrimage bolster the pilgrims faith in the Unity of Allah.

5. Pilgrimage is also a reminder of the satanic traps. The satanic pillars at Mina where pebbles are thrown by the pilgrims, bring to their mind the single minded devotion of Ibrahim in the way of Allah.

6. Pilgrimage imparts a singular lesson in religious faith and morality. Beside other virtues it fosters in the pilgrims love of Allah, perseverance, resignation to Divine Will, contentment, trust in Allah, suppression of lust for material wealth, fellow-feeling and equality.

Necessary details in regard to the pilgrimage have been discussed above. It would be altogether senseless to assert that one who disregards this act of prayer can still lead a religious life. If a Muslim entertains such disregard for the pilgrimage he is devoid of religious spirit. If in spite of having sufficient means, a Muslim is not attracted to this centre of religion, the edifice of his faith will remain incomplete. On the contrary, if a Muslim performs this devotion to the best of his ability, he doubtlessly constructs the edifice of his faith on the most firm foundation.

A Collective View of the Pillars of Islam

The fundamental duties of Islam have been discussed at length in the foregoing chapters. Their nature, significance and true characteristics have been highlighted therein. A thoughtful study would lead one to the conclusion that these are not merely the acts but the very fountainheads of worship and goodness. Each act plays a vital role in invoking a sense of submission to Allah and in its perfection. Each act plays a role of its own and cannot be substituted by another. Jointly they forge a frame of mind that finds a complete satisfaction in Islam. They bestow upon him a heart that seeks nothing but Divine Will. They give him a spirit which ceaselessly struggles for Divine pleasure. Thus prepared for submission unto Allah he is always on the ready to comply with His injunctions. Through constant labour his heart is so cultured that no religious guidance goes waste in its soil. It readily accepts the seed sown in it and starts the process of nourishing it. In view of their basic importance the Prophet *s.a.w.* regarded these acts as "pillars of Islam". The whole edifice of the Faith rests upon them. It is a simile which best expresses their significance in the religion of Islam.

11

ISLAM AS A WAY OF LIFE

After understanding the fundamental beliefs and acts of Islam let us now study its entire way of life. As leaves correspond to their seed, the teachings of a religion are identical to its basic concept. In other words, the teachings of a religion are a reflection of its basic concept. In order to understand the full scope of Islamic teachings it is but necessary that we know its religious concept.

Various Concepts of Religion

Three concepts of religion are prevalent in the present day world:

i.   According, to one concept this world is a prison-house. Man's body is like a cage. His own passions constitute its bars. One can only find release from this prison-house when one demolishes its walls. His soul will be emancipated if he breaks its bars with his own hands. It means that he should renounce the world, abandon the populace and take refuge in solitude for establishing communion with God. He should suppress his desires, or better still, crush them completely. Thus he would remove the veil which shrouds his vision and obstructs his access to God. This situation makes it obligatory that he gets rid of this world.

This concept of religion and worship is known as "Asceticism" or "Yoga"

ii.   The second concept does not require, renunciation and self-mortification. It enjoins the worship of God and allows, within reasonable limits, the fulfilment of instinctive human desires and immoral activities. So far as individual life is concerned religion gives definite injunctions one has to abide by. Beyond his individual life he enjoys complete freedom. This concept regards worship a private affair that has no concern with society. Religion, as such, is a matter between God and the individual. It does not interfere in man's social life. In his temporal life man is free to choose whatever course he likes. He is at liberty to adopt whatever system he chooses. Religion and God do not interfere with his choice and liking.

iii. The third concept of religion considers the renunciation of world and self-mortification as wrong. It rejects the idea that worship is an individual affair and religion a private matter. According to this concept the truth is quite otherwise. Whether it is a place of worship, a house, a farm, a marketplace or a political forum, wherever a man may be, he performs a religious duty and an act of worship. He can neither abandon any of these places nor can he do as he wishes. Whatever faculties he is endowed with are meant for acts of worship. Neither of these faculties is to be destroyed nor can he do as he wishes. Whatever faculties he is endowed with are meant for acts of worship. Neither of these faculties is to be destroyed nor left unbridled. The true faith and worship lies in leading individual as well as collective life in consonance with the Divine injunctions. If he worships Allah in a sacred place he should also do the same outside it. Wherever he is he should do what Allah has ordained. His temporal life should conform to the injunctions of his Master.

Asceticism Not Permitted in Islam

Islam does not accord with the first of these concepts of religion. Every constituent of Islam contradicts it. Foremost in this contradiction are the practical beliefs and fundamental duties discussed in the previous chapters. They make it abundantly clear that:

(a) In Islam the concept of Allah is not of a "Real Beloved" alone.

It also accepts Him as his "Real Master" and "Law-Maker". Obviously the concept of renunciation can only be true if He is only a "Beloved and Sought-after object" and nothing else. But when the factual position is quite different and He is man's Ruler and Law-Maker also, it implies that He must be having some kind of laws and injunctions as well for His subjects. It does not therefore, suffice that man should be lost in the fear and remembrance of Allah. It is equally important that he should enter the field of Life and prove himself His obedient subject by his submission to the Divine Commands.

(b) For the proper performance of such principal duties, as constitute the pillar of the edifice of Islam, some kind of social life is indispensable. Needless to say that an ascetic life has no such element. In a way of life that does not make even the performance of principal duties of Islam possible, practice of Islam in full is out of question.

(c) These pillars of Islam are in fact in the nature of prayer but at the same time they have in their fold many of the social values and national expediencies of religion. This is why Islam so emphatically requires that they should be performed collectively and not individually. On the one side it proves that the character of Islam, as portrayed by its fundamental duties, is not consonant with the practice of self-mortification and asceticism. On the other side it shows that if a person performs the daily prayers and pays Zakat (poor-due) in isolation these acts will not yield the result Islam aims to attain through them. In such a situation, what to say of more, even to the extent of these prayers, the single purpose of worship of Allah will not be attained in full.

(d) The five principal duties of Islam have been designated as the pillars of Islam and not the "complete Islam". It clearly means that Islam is not the name of these five articles only. There are other things also which constitute its essential components. In spite of the vital importance of the pillars and their paramount significance, it cannot be denied that a building does not comprise of pillars and walls only. Nor any number of pillars have ever been called a building. A building comes to be considered as such when its walls are covered with a ceiling. In other words walls and roof together form a building. The building of Islam must have its roof also of which these five principal duties would form the pillars. When put together they would acquire the shape of a building. The roof of Islam would be the teachings beside the five duties discussed above. It is a well known fact that among these teachings a large number concern the practical life. Their practice in isolation is as difficult as swimming in sand. So even if it is presumed that the practice of the fundamental duties of Islam is possible in seclusion it does not mean that it would amount to doing full justice to the observance of Islam. Doing full justice to the five principal duties is one thing and practising Islam in full measure is quite another. Fulfilment of these five principal duties could only be considered complete adherence to Islam if it comprised nothing beside them. But in the light or the above discussion there is no room for any such consideration.

All these facts which are contained in the fundamentals of Islam make it clear that Islam has nothing to do with asceticism nor is asceticism related to Islam.

The following quotations would support this contention. The Holy Prophet *s.a.w.* said:

"There is no place for asceticism in Islam" (*Nail al-Autar*).

When 'Uthman bin Maz'un sought permission from the Holy Prophet *s.a.w.* for getting himself castrated, he refused and said:

"In place of asceticism Allah has bestowed upon us an easier course and the religion of Abraham. (*Tabarani*)

Similarly the Christians, who had begun to consider asceticism as the zenith of piety and Godliness were censured by Allah.

They have taken to asceticism on their own. We have not ordained it for them. (57:27)

It means that Islam is not alone in condemning asceticism. Other divine religions also do not allow it. Whoever adopted this course did it on his own. No Divine religion has ever been in concord with the philosophy of asceticism.

As Divine religion is opposed to asceticism and its fundamental beliefs and duties evince their keen discord for it, so do its teachings. This is why the Holy Prophet *s.a.w.* prohibited every such act which had any similarity with asceticism or led to it. Acts such as celibacy, castration, permanent fasting, abstinence from food after fast, self-imposed silence, nocturnal vigils which deprive one's body of rest and rob his family of their genuine rights, are strictly forbidden accordingly.

Islam Does Not Cover Individual Life Only

The second concept of religion is also not in agreement with Islam. It is not a type of religion which regards the link between God and man a personal matter. Had it been so, its teachings would be restricted to the problems of individual life only. It would, in that case, speak only of the mosque, prescribe the fast, lay down some morals and ethics and nothing beyond that. But every page of the Qur'an and the Tradition bears evidence that it is not so. Islam does not prescribe laws for prayer and personal life only. It governs every field of man's activity and legislates injunctions and prohibitions in every sphere of life be it economic, cultural, political, official or any other. Nothing is outside its scope. For instance the Qur'an prescribes a hundred stripes for an adulterer. This injunction concerns the police, the judiciary and the government. It is clearly a social affair. But according to the Qur'an this injunction is "Religion of Allah".

And let not pity for the twain withhold you from the obedience (Religion) of Allah (24:2).

It means that according to the Qur'an the order of serving a hundred stripes to an adulterer is a part of the religion of Allah and not something outside it. Similarly the Qur'an says that four months of a year are sacred and waging of war is not permissible during these months. Obviously this commandment of the Qur'an relates to the laws of war, which again is one of the problems of man's social life. But the Qur'an regards this also the "Right Religion".

Four of them (months) are sacred: That is the straight religion (9:36).

The order that the sacredness of these four months should be maintained and the injunction that their sanctity is not violated by war are a part of religion and not something outside its jurisdiction.

The Qur'an does not hold its own social laws as "religion" but also regards the social laws of other religions and societies as "their religions". This is why in the narrative of the Prophet Yusuf [Joseph] (*a.s.*) the Qur'an uses the following words:

He could not have taken his brother according to the king's Din (religion) (12:76).

It was not possible for the Prophet Yusuf (*a.s.*) to detain his brother under "the *Din* (religion) of the king of Egypt" signifies nothing except the laws of his land, the criminal code of his country.

These examples are suffcent to make it clear that each order of Allah and every saying of the Prophet Muhammad *s.a.w.* is a part of Islam and a constituent of religion. None of them is to be deemed outside the realm of religion.

Even logically it is not a sound proposition. If Islam signifies an unqualified submission to Allah, how can any of His orders be regarded outside the sphere of submission? How can some of His

orders be treated outside the realm of religion and their compliance
not considered compulsory.

The above discussion brings us to the conclusion that the Qur'an
and the Tradition contain injunctions covering all spheres of man's
life, individual as well as social, and each of these injunctions is but
an integral part of Islam. In the face of these facts is it possible to
think and say that Islam covers individual life only? Is it a religion
which has no concern with the social problems of man?

Islam: A Complete Code of Life

If at a given time it is accepted that it is not night, then it would go
without saying that it is day-time. Similarly, when it is established
that Islam neither endorses asceticism nor it covers the problem of
individual life alone, then its character is determined automatically.
It is implied that no problem is outside its scope. It is a religion
which dominates man's entire life. He meets its legislation at every
step. In short it is a code which governs every aspect of his life-be
it religious, intellectual, moral, practical or any other. It can be
compared to the air which encompasses the planet of earth. In the
following passages will be found a brief outline of its essential
constituents. These would, on the one hand, prove the contention put
forth heretofore and, on the other, throw light on what this system
really is? It seems advisable to have a firm grasp of the following
basic principles:

1.   Every constituent of this system is connected with its centre.
      One and the same spirit breathes in all of them. This centre and
      this spirit are the articles of faith and belief which have already
      been discussed in the second chapter of this book. Among these
      the belief that Allah alone is to be worshipped, He alone is our
      real Master and true Legislator, is of supreme importance. In
      fact this is the fundamental belief, the root of the entire system
      of Islam. In order to understand the significance of any
      constituent of this system it is indispensable that it is studied in

full.

2. The implementation of this system is contingent upon a society which is Muslim. A society which has deep faith in Allah and His attributes, sincerely believes in the Afterlife and wholeheartedly believes in the Prophethood of Muhammad *s.a.w.* and accepts him as the Last of His Prophets. In short it is a society which is a true follower of Islam. For the proper evaluation of this system it is but essential that it should be studied in relation to an Islamic Society. It is impossible to appreciate the finish and sharpness of a sword unless one is an expert fencer. Similarly, in the absence of a true Islamic society the correct evaluation of Islamic System is impossible.

3. Different parts of this system are as closely connected with each other as different parts of a machine. For the purpose of visual perception they can be divided into separate compartments but in function their independent existence is out of question. In actual practice all these constituents are one. Practical merit of any of these comes into play when the whole system is at work. Not only this, even the proper understanding of one constituent is not possible unless the others are also in view.

Keeping in mind the principles stated above let us now proceed to study the Islamic system.

1. SPIRITUAL SYSTEM

The nucleus of the Islamic system is the part which has a direct bearing on the inner life of a man. It is commonly known as the spiritual system and strives to emancipate his spirit from the servitude of "self", purges it of the lust of worldly life and imbues it with the passion of His love, obedience and pleasure. A person attains the required level of purity and passion when he identifies his own likes and dislikes with that of Allah. He acts upon the commands of his real Master as if he is seeing Him with his own eyes, fears His displeasure as if he is in His presence, actively pursues His pleasure as one burning with thirst makes a rush for water. He is always on the ready to sacrifice his life and wealth, as all humble offering on His slightest biddings. This level of spiritualism, which represents the loftiest and the best standard, is known as "Ihsan" in Islamic terms.

The methods prescribed by Islam for attaining this level of purity and Divine pleasure are called "the pillars of Islam". They have been discussed at length earlier under the heading "Fundamental Acts". How do the prayer, the Zakat (poor-due), the fast and the pilgrimage inculcate such a frame of mind? This question has also been dealt with in previous chapters and needs no repetition.

2.   MORAL SYSTEM

The initial and the most popular means of evaluating the piety or otherwise of one's spirit is by appraising one's moral behaviour. Outward conduct is but an index of one's inward life. The moral standards of a person reflect his humanity. This is why, in order of merit, next to spiritual system comes the moral system. This contention is also endorsed by religion as it attaches a high degree of importance to the decency of behaviour. So much so that in one respect it is the essence of religion. The Prophet Muhammad *s.a.w.* said:

> "I have been sent for the perfection of civilised behaviour" (*Muwatta*).

> Piety is the name of decent behaviour (*Muslim*).

It is for this particular reason that Islam has dealt with the moral system at length and laid so much emphasis on it. Hence there is justification for prior study of this constituent of Islamic system.

In this connection one must first know the nature of Islamic Society. Has Islam classified good and bad morals? If yes, have they been so declared for ever or there is a possibility of change in them because of temporal ups and downs? These questions can be answered easily. Islam possesses an authority for making such a judgement about morals. This authority rests with Allah and His Prophet Muhammad *s.a.w.*. It is this authority alone which determines the morality or immorality of each and every act. That is why it is a settled issue in Islam and is not open to the judgement or wisdom of any one. It is an admitted fact that some degree of moral has always been in force in human society. It is not therefore peculiar to Islam. But, nevertheless, it would be a blunder to treat the Islamic morality and, any mundane morality on the same footing because Islam has not declared any act as good or bad for the reason that people have considered it to be so for a long time or its importance has been reinforced by wisdom and experience. Islam judges an act according to its own principles. This is why a huge number of Islamic morals are the same as are approved on all hands. But at the same time we come across some such, things in Islamic morality which Islam considers good and virtuous but they are treated differently by others. Conversely there are certain things which Islam regards as vicious and bad but these are treated as virtuous by many. It goes to prove that Islam has its own standard and permanent system in regard to morals. Its judgement in respect of morals is based upon its own principles and character. Since the Islamic morals have a permanent base, and have emerged from its fundamental principles, they are unchangeable and everlasting. No circumstances can have any effect on them. Truth and honesty shall always remain the highest virtues; justice, will be done even if it harms one's own interest; violation of promise is not permissible even with one's enemy. In short these morals have an abiding value and are not susceptible to any change whatsoever. Such is the character of Islamic morals. Keeping this character of Islamic morals in view, let us proceed on their survey. First of all we take up morals which are of fundamental importance and concern our day-to-day life. Allah has ordained:

Be thou kind as Allah hath been kind to thee (28:77).

Those who control their wrath and are forgiving towards mankind (3:134).

Allah loveth not each treacherous ingrate (22:38).

And squander not (thy wealth) in wantonness (17:26).

Turn not thy cheek in scorn towards folk, nor walk with pertiness in the land. Lo! Allah loveth not each braggart boaster (31:18).

Woe unto every slandering traducer (104:1).

The Prophet Muhammad *s.a.w.* said:

"Undoubtedly truthfulness leads to piety and piety leads to heaven—and falsehood leads to vice and that shows the way to hell" (*Bukhari and Muslim*).

Even a modicum of ostentation is unbelief (*Mishkat*).

"Save yourself from cruelty because cruelty will take shape of whirlwind on the Day of Reckoning" (*Muslim*).

"He who has the four vices in him is a confirmed hypocrite. A person who possesses one of these vices has one quality of hypocrisy. These four vices are:

1. He who breaches the trust when some security has been entrusted to him.

2. He who tells lies when he speaks.

3. He who does not keep his promise.

4. He who uses filthy language in a quarrel. (*Muslim*)

    "Acquire politeness and keep away from rudeness and indecent language" (*Muslim*).

    "Backbiters shall be deprived of heaven" (*Muslim*).

    "Allah shall not show mercy to him who does not take pity on his fellow-beings" (*Bukhari*).

"The cheat, the miser and the one who reminds his beneficiaries of his kindness to them shall not enter heaven" (*Tirmidhi*).

After studying these basic morals of Islam we come to such moral injunctions which Islam has enjoined for special spheres of life.

1.   The first sphere of man is his own home where he has to deal with his wife and children. Everyone has a natural affection for them and makes sacrifices for their sake. According to Islam it is not an instinctive urge only. It is a religious obligation as well. Allah commands:

Consort with them in kindness (4:19).

The Prophet Muhammad *s.a.w.* has said:

"Among you the best are those who are good to their wives" (*Tirmidhi*).

"In respect of women accept the advice: Treat them well" (*Bukhari* and *Muslim*).

2.   Next to one's home comes the sphere of one's family life where he comes into contact with his parents, brothers, sisters and other near relatives. The importance of the attitude which one has to adopt with his parents can be judged from the fact that Allah has ordained it in the same injunction wherein He has enjoined the prayer:

And serve Allah. Ascribe nothing as partner unto Him, (Show) kindness unto parents (4:36).

And lower unto them the wings of submission through mercy and say: My Lord! Have mercy on them as they did care for me when I was little (17:24),

From what the Prophet *s.a.w.* has said in this respect we quote here two of his sayings:

"Your parents are your heaven and hell" (*Ibn Majah*).

"To such noble children as cast an affectionate glance on their
parents, Allah grants the reward of one approved pilgrimage for
each of their glances" (*Baihaqi*).

So much so that if parents of a Muslim happen to be non-
Muslims or even avowed enemies of Islam the rights of their service
and obedience will remain unaltered. Islam enjoins that their rights
are to be fulfilled:

Consort with them in the world kindly (36:15).

As for the other relatives are concerned the Qur'an enjoins a
universal good treatment to all of them. In the above mentioned
surah "an-Nisa" (Women) of the Qur'an the words which
immediately follow the verse "*(Show) kindness unto parents*"(4:36).
There occur the following words: *And unto near kindred* (4:36).

These words signify that as one should consort with his parents
because of their being the closest relatives, similarly one should treat
his other relations according to the closeness of their relationship with
him. Such relatives as have closer relationship with him have a
greater claim on him.

"First duty of yours, is that to your mother then that to your father, and then to near (of your relatives)" (*Bukhari*).

A Muslim is obliged to treat each one of his relatives in
accordance with this principle.

Good treatment of one's relatives is technically known as
SilaturRahim. It means the maintenance and support of blood
relationship. The Qur'an has regarded it as the foundation stone of
humanity and piousness and duly emphasised it. The Prophet
Muhammad *s.a.w.* has counted it among the requirements of faith.

"He who believes in Allah and the After-life must show kindness to his relatives" (*Bukhari*).

"He who breaks the blood relationship shall not enter into

heaven" (*Bukhari*).

3.   After the family, comes the sphere of neighbourhood. How a Muslim should treat his neighbour is evident from the following two traditions:

> "The Angel Gabriel so repeatedly advised me about the rights of the neighbours that I began to think that my neighbour is meant to be my heir" (*Bukhari*).

> "A person whose neighbour is not safe from his excesses will not enter heaven" (*Muslim*).

4.   Next to neighbours comes the vast sphere of social life in which one has to deal with different types of people. How one should behave with them? The Qur'an provides us an answer to this question in the following words:

> *(Show) kindness unto parents and unto near kindred, and orphans and the needy and unto the neighbourer who is of him (unto you) and unto neighbours who is not of him, and the fellow traveller and the way-farer and the slaves* (4:36).

This verse has enumerated all the relations a man can possibly have. It contains a comprehensive advice that a Muslim should be kind and well-meaning in his treatment with them.

5.   After the mundane social life comes the sphere of Government in an Islamic society the position of an individual also is predetermined from social and administrative angles. Each individual is so placed that he is either in a position to command or obey. He is either a ruler or the ruled. How has he to behave with his subordinates is evident from the following saying of the Prophet *s.a.w.*:

> "He who is entrusted with the responsibility to lead the Muslims but does not suffer hardship for them, nor thinks of their betterment will not enter the Paradise" (*Muslim*).

How a subject should behave with his ruler is also made clear in the following tradition:

"The Prophet *s.a.w.* said: The religion means sincerity and loyalty. When he was asked whose sincerity and loyalty, he replied, sincerity to Allah, His Prophet and Chiefs of the Muslims and all the Muslims" (*Muslim*).

It means that it is an essential requirement of piety and fear of Allah that the treatment of the subjects by their rulers, and the behaviour of the subjects towards their rulers, is based on sincerity and good-will.

6.   Last of all comes the sphere where a Muslim has to deal with the people outside the Muslim Society. What should be his conduct while dealing with non-Muslims is given in the under-mentioned verse of the Qur'an:

O ye who believe! Be steadfast witness for Allah in equity, and let not hatred of any people seduce you that ye deal not justly. Deal justly that is nearer to your piety (5:8).

These are the fundamental principles on which Islam constructs the moral life of man. Their study would reveal that every fibre of a Muslim's life is subject to strict moral laws.

Family Laws

After discussing the two fields of fundamental importance let us proceed to study the structure of the society and examine Islamic injunctions in regard to each of them.

The civic or social structure emerges from the companionship of a man and a woman. The social circle which comes into existence with this companionship forms the first link of the social order. This social circle is called family life and the laws which govern it are known as family laws. The redeeming features of the family laws framed by Islam are as follows.

This permanent companionship of a man and a woman emerges from an open contract which is known in technical terms as "Nikah" (marriage). It is a sacred relation which is formed with the mutual consent of the two partners and through, an open declaration. The relation of a man with any woman is otherwise a sin of the worst kind and calls for the most severe punishment. Marriage is not only a physical necessity but also a religious requirement

"Marry with the women, whosoever avoid my Sunnah does not belong to me" (*Bukhari*).

Keeping oneself aloof from this requirement is contrary to Islam:

"Allah's Messenger (peace and blessings of Allah be upon him) rejected the proposal of Uthman bin Mazun to lead the life of celibacy" (*Bukhari*).

The contract of marriage is described as a "strong pledge" (4:36) in the Qur'an. Owing to this contract the twain accepts certain heavy responsibilities. They accept these responsibilities permanently. This contract gives rise to a social unity. Man is its supervisor and administrator and woman carries out its affairs under his guidance.

Men are in charge of women (4:34).

In this social unity man is entrusted with the following responsibilities:

1.   He has to provide for his wife and children. This means food, clothing, living, in short, all the necessities of His responsibility to provide them with the necessities of life would be in proportion to his means:

Let him who hath in abundance spend of his abundance and whose provision is measured let him spend that which Allah hath given him (66:7).

This responsibility is not moral. It is legal and obligatory. If someone neglects it the government would compel him fulfil it.

2.   He has to impart religious training and education to wife and children:

O ye who believe! ward off from yourself and your families a fire, thereof the fuel is men and stones (66:7)

In short in man is reposed the twofold responsibility of providing the worldly needs to his family and to be mindful of their welfare in the Afterlife.

Every one of you is answerable for his subject. Man is guardian of his family and is answerable for his subject (Agreed upon).

A married woman is the guardian of her husband's family and is answerable for that (Agreed upon).

So good women are the obedient, guarding in secret that which Allah hath guarded (4:34).

Similarly, it is the duty of the children to serve and obey their parents. Disobedience on their part is an unpardonable sin:

"Allah would pardon whatever sin He would like to pardon except the disobedience to parents" (Mishkat).

Marriage is thus a religious obligation. The responsibilities accruing from it have been regarded in the Qur'an as "the limits imposed by Allah"

These are the limits(imposed by) Allah (2:229)

Men and women both have been enjoined to keep these limits. Every gentleman and dutiful person is expected to observe these limits. But if, God forbid, the limits are not kept and differences crop up between a married couple and no hope is left for a compromise, there is a provision for the termination of this contract through divorce. Man can have recourse to what is technically called "Talaq" and woman to "Khull".

And if ye fear that they may not be able to keep the limits of

Allah, in that case there is no sin for either if woman ransom herself (2:229).

Even the government has the power to intervene in such a situation and break the marriage. In view of the importance of marriage this provision may appear strange but in Islam nothing can exceed the sanctity of the limits prescribed by Allah. The marriage cannot be maintained by transgressing the limits of Allah.

3. SOCIAL SYSTEM

Beyond the limited sphere of home lies a vast collective social life which is known as society. Islam has also laid down some fundamental principles in respect of this sphere. Let us acquaint ourselves with the basic concepts of the Islamic social system. Their detailed study would be taken up subsequently.

According to Islam the multitude of people, who collectively form a society, are off-springs of one parentage:

Who created you from a single soul (4:1).

As such they are all equal by birth. There is neither a difference of high and low, nor of pure and impure. People of every colour, ciime and race are equal in status and rights.

There cannot be any distinction among them because of any peculiarity of colour, race, country or language. Only one thing can be group of men who has faith in the religion of Allah. There is another which does not have faith in it. The former is called Islamic society and the latter is known as un-Islamic or infidel society. Evidently their basic premises are quite different. When their premises are different their structures must also follow suit. In major affairs of life there is no similarity among them. For example, the relationship of marriage which is the corner-stone of social system, cannot be established between Muslims and non-Muslims. Nor can they become heirs of each other.

Thus on the basis of faith and religion emerge two permanent societies. Naturally Islam has separate injunctions for each of them. As for the non-Muslims society is concerned it is the essence of teachings that its members should be treated in usual manner. In their dealings with them, the Muslims cannot make any exception in matters like justice and equity, honesty and trustworthiness, compassion and kindness, uprightness and promise. In respect of Islamic society, Islam has given express injunctions. These injunctions form "the Social System of Islam". Here is the gist of these injunctions:

1.   Instead of any class war or tribal rancour the mutual relations of Muslims are based on brotherhood, sympathy, co-operation and sacrifice. There is a Divine injunction that:

The believers are naught else than brothers (49:10).

What kind of "brotherhood" this is in actual practice is elucidated in the following verse:

But give them preference over their selves even when they themselves are needy (59:6).

Let not a folk deride a folk;

Nor let women deride women;

Neither defame one another, nor insult one another by nick-names;

Shun much suspicion and spy not, neither backbite one another (49:11-12).

"Muslims are like a building, each constituent of which is a support for the other" (Bukhari).

"In respect of natural love, compassion and kindness, Muslims are like a body which is in fever and feel discomfort if any of its part is ailing" (*Bukhari*).

"Do not be envious of each other. Nor give a higher bid in auction to raise the price, nor foster any ill-will against each other, nor abandon contacts with each other, nor interfere in the sale deeds of others to promote your own interest--but be a good bondsman of Allah and treat each other as brothers. Each Muslim is a brother unto other. Neither he makes any excesses on the other nor leaves him helpless in lurch, nor looks down upon him. It is the bounden duty of each Muslim to respect the blood, property and honour of every Muslim" (*Muslim*).

"Every Muslim has six obligations towards another Muslim:

(i)   When a Muslim meets another he should salute him in the prescribed manner;

(ii) When a Muslim cries for help he should assist him;

(iii) When a Muslim seeks advice from another he should give him;

(iv) When a Muslim sneezes and says *Al Hamdu Lillah* (Allah be praised) the other Muslim should follow his prayer and say: *Yarhamuka-Allah* (Allah have mercy on you);

(v)   When a Muslim falls sick he should visit and inquire about his health;

(vi) When a Muslim dies he should attend his funeral". (*Muslim*)

"It is not permissible for a Muslim that he abandons his brother for more than three days" (*Bukhari*).

"No Muslim should send a proposal of marriage to woman whose hand has already been or is being sought by someone else, till the first party either marries or refuses. (*Bukhari*)

"Beware of such things as estrangement or mutual relations because they are capable of sweeping the religion away" (*Tirmidhi*).

Such is the nature of mutual relationship amongst people in a Muslim society. Whenever this state of love and brotherhood is found in danger because of any misunderstanding or selfishness, it is obligatory for others that they rush for redeeming the situation.

The believers are naught else than brothers. Therefore make peace between your brethren (49:10) .

It is stated in a tradition that the Prophet Muhammad *s.a.w.* said to his companions Allah be pleased with them):

"May I tell you something which is higher than fasting, alms giving and prayer? The companions said, "Please do let us know about it". He said, "It is keeping your mutual relations cordial" (Tirmidhi).

2.   Virtues such as welfare of people and fear of Allah be encouraged in the society. These should not only be encouraged but people should co-operate with each other in such noble acts:

Help ye one another unto righteousness and piousness (5:2).

Even this is not enough. People should actually incite each other for such acts:

And the believers, men and women, are protecting friends one of another, they enjoin the right (9:71).

3.   Vices should not be allowed to flourish in the society. The right course to achieve this end, is that on the one hand no one should be helped in an evil deed:

Help not one another unto sin and transgression (5:2).

On the other hand one should do one's best to keep the people away from evils:

"Whosoever amongst you sees evil, he should check it with the help of his hand" (*Bukhari*).

Keeping the people away from evils is not only a service and betterment of the society, it is also a service and betterment of the person who is being prevented from doing it. The Prophet Muhammad once advised:

"Help your brother whether he is aggressor or the victim of aggression".

On hearing this advice his companions (r.a.) inquired from him s.a.w.:

"O Prophet of Allah! We can make out the reason for helping the aggressed but we cannot understand how an aggressor should be helped?" He replied: "You should stop him from aggression because that amounts to his help" (Bukhari).

4.   All such sources should be sealed up which cause an inflow of sexual evils in the society. The following measures have been employed for this purpose:

(a)   Adultery is listed among the worst of the sins:

And whoso doeth this shall meet the punishment of his sin (25:68).

The whole society is charged with intense hatred against this sin.

The adulterer shall not marry save an adulteress or an idolatress, and the adulteress none shall marry save an adulterer or idolator (26:3).

(b)   Punishment prescribed for one who is guilty of adultery is equally terrible. He is stoned to death or is scourged with a hundred stripes. It is also provided that this punishment should be inflicted in public and maximum number of persons should witness it. The executioner of the punishment should not show any leniency in doing his duty:

*And let no pity for the twain take hold of you, and let a party of
the believers witness their punishment* (24:2).

In general circumstances the women's sphere of work is limited
to their homes and they have been prohibited to turn out:

And stay in your houses (33:33).

Free mixing of men and women is strictly forbidden. With the
exception of such relatives as are very close to them, women are not
permitted to come in the presence of men unveiled.

Draw their cloaks close round them (when they go abroad)
(33:59).

Similarly women have also been enjoined not to come out
perfumed. Nor are they permitted to use such ornaments which produce sound while walking when they go out. They are also enjoined
not to talk unnecessarily with the men who are not very close
relatives. When they are obliged to do so, they should not speak with
them in a soft tone:

*Be not soft of speech, lest in whose heart is a disease aspire (to
you)* (33:32).

(c) Muslim women are strictly forbidden the use of such
garments which are worn for display or effect. Same is true
of their manners. Such women have been cursed who wear
clothes which reveal their body. Also cursed are the women
who walk with a swinging gait.

"Women who would be naked in spite of being dressed they
would be inclined to evil and make their husbands inclined
towards it; their heads would be like humps of *bhukht* camel
inclined toward one side. They will not enter Paradise and
would not smell its odour" (*Muslim*).

(d) Shame and modesty are strongly commanded and have
been declared constituents of faith:

"Modesty is a branch of faith" (*Bukhari*).

(e) Muslim men and women are enjoined not to focus their eyes on their opposite sex when they come across them. Instead they should lower their eyes in such an event:

Tell the believing men to lower their gaze and be modest. And tell the believing women to lower their gaze and be modest, and not to display of their adornment except that which is apparent (24:30-31).

(f) Similarly the Muslims, both men and women, have been ordained not to enter anyone's house without announcement and permission

O ye who believe! Enter not houses other than your own without first announcing your presence and invoking peace upon the folk thereof (24:27).

(g) Propagation of evil is strictly forbidden as it injures the intellectual modesty of the society and weakens the natural hatred of people against that evil. Those who do so have been warned of severe punishment:

"There is forgiveness for every one of my followers except one who spreads obscenity" (*Bukhari*).

Those who want to see society inclined to obscenity have been reprimanded in the Qur'an:

Lo! Those who love that slander should be spread concerning those who believe, there will be a painful punishment for them in the world and the Hereafter (24:19).

(h) Marriage is enjoined and celibacy of young men is pointedly condemned:

"Whosoever amongst you can afford to marry he must marry for it makes man modest and chaste" (Mishkat).

It is ordained that when a girl comes of age she should be married immediately on the availability of a suitable match:

"When one of you gives you the proposal of marriage whose religion and behaviour please, you then marry him but if you do not do that, then it may be source Of wide spread corruption on the earth" (Tirmidhi).

Islam has also made the institution of marriage simple and convenient. Except for very close relatives marriage is permissible with all others. Difference of caste is also no bar for marriage. It is said:

"In marriage people usually go after caste and family, beauty and riches but you Muslims should only see the faith and conduct" (*Mishkat*).

"Look unto his religion" (*Mishkat*).

In respect of dowry and gift Muslims have been ordained to adopt a middle course. Similarly marriage ceremony has also been made so plain that one does not feel any inconvenience in it. Neither one needs a priest for it nor an officer. Nor is it subject to any other condition. The twain can perform the ceremony themselves by giving their consent in the presence of two witnesses. This would suffice for the purpose.

In certain moral or social exigencies one is also permitted to make up to four marriages. This permission is subject to condition that he would be just to each of them. For example, it would be quite justified if it is done for the sake of an orphan who cannot be brought up without being taken as a foster child. It would also be valid if a person finds himself unable to be content with one wife:

Marry of the women, who seem good to you, two or three or four (4:3).

Widow and widowers have been advised to start their matrimonial life afresh. Similar injunctions exist for slaves of either sex. Whoever of them is fit for marriage should be married:

"And marry such of you as are solitary and the pious of your slaves and maidservants" (24:32).

This has been ordained for the reason that no one in the society who is sexually potent, leads a life of celibacy. If he is neglected he may succumb to some sin.

5.   Islam also restrains from such entertainments which incline a man to debauchery and licentiousness or impair his intellectual powers and paralyse his moral sense. This accounts for the prohibition of all such things as dance, music, liquor and other intoxicants in Islam.

6.   As regards the style of living and eating, Islam exhorts nothing but moderation. According to the definition given in the Qur'an, a Muslim is neither extravagant nor miserly in spending

And those who, when they spend are neither prodigal nor grudging and there is a moderate position between the two (25:67).

It would be relevant to quote here two sayings of the Prophet *s.a.w.* on this subject. He *s.a.w.* said:

"Allah wants to see the effect of His blessings on His slave" (*Muslim*).

At the same time Allah has strictly forbidden a living that is ostentatious, luxurious and extravagant. For instance wearing of such a dress is not permissible which is so very low as to touch the ground by way of pride:

"He who drags his cloth (lower garment) out of pride, Allah will not look at him (with Mercy) on the Day of Resurrection" (Mishkat).

Similarly the use of gold and silver ornaments is not allowed. Men are not permitted to wear silken clothes or sit upon silken mat:

"The Messenger of Allah prohibited us to eat or drink in gold or silver utensils and to use the silken fabrics for dress or bed" (Mishkat).

One should have only such household goods as are essential for one's use:

"One bed for husband, the other for wife, the third for guest and the fourth is for Satan" (Muslim).

Construction of huge and high mansions is also not viewed with favour. The Prophet *s.a.w.* said:

"Every expense that a Muslim makes on himself is in fact an expenditure in the way of Allah, except for expense incurred on buildings exceeding one's own requirements as there is nothing good in them" (Tirmidhi).

Muslims have also been told to avoid a luxurious life:

"Beware of luxurious living for Allah does not like those who have taken to luxurious living" (Mishkat).

7.   The natural capabilities of men and women are as different as their spheres of activities. Their appearance and dress should also be likewise different. The Prophet *s.a.w.* has ordained:

"Allah has cursed such men who acquire the appearance of women, and also woman who imitate men" (*Bukhari*).

8.   Muslims should never lose their grip over forbearance, grace and serenity. The death of a relative is very trying but one is enjoined not to give way to impatience and crying even in that event:

"One should not slap one's face or raise fulsome lamentation, or tear one's clothes or dishevel one's hair" (Abu Dawud).

Similarly one should not feel overjoyed in the event of great happiness:

Nor ye exult because of that which hath been given (57:23).

Islamic injunctions do not ordain only such virtues as patience, grace and serenity, they also enjoin the observance of pleasing habits. It enjoins:

"Do not eat with the left hand" (*Muslim*).

"Do not clean private parts with your right hand. It would be still better if you do not even touch your private parts with your right hand" (*Bukhari*).

"Do not walk with one foot covered and the other uncovered" (*Muslim*).

Do not shave a part of your head:

"The Prophet of Allah *s.a.w.* has forbidden to shave a part of one's head" (*Bukhari*).

9.   Muslims have been forbidden such acts as are devoid of any consequence here or in the Hereafter. Among the basic virtues of a Muslim listed in the Qur'an one is that he does not have any concern with futile deeds:

And who shuns all that which is vain (18:3).

The Prophet *s.a.w.* has said:

"One or the hallmarks of a Muslim is that he keeps himself aloof from useless things" (*Tirmidhi*).

10. Islam forbids such acts as are earmarked for some un-Islamic society and are likely to impair the cultural identity and religious temper of the Muslims. For instance it is ordained that:

(a) No Muslim should fashion himself in the style of nonbelievers otherwise he would be reckoned one of them.

"He who imitates a people is one of them" (*Abu Dawud*).

(b) The Muslims should have beards and moustaches of the style opposite to the non-Muslims:

"Oppose the non-believers, grow beards and trim moustaches" (*Bukhari*).

(c) The Christians and the Jews keep their hair undyed, so oppose them.

"The Muslims are advised to do otherwise" (*Bukhari*).

In short, the temper of the Muslim society is attuned to righteousness and uniformity that they are distinguished in each and every respect. For them all such so-called liberal views which regard that essentially there is a good deal in common between belief and unbelief, is sheer flattery and deceit. Islam believes that white is different from the black. It strongly refutes any idea that the two have anything in common.

4.   ECONOMIC SYSTEM

Any one who has some knowledge of Islam knows that the real interest of a Muslim lies not in this world but in the Hereafter. That is the sole object he lives and dies for. It is a mark of distinction for a Muslim that he prefers the After-life to this world and concentrates his attention accordingly. This is something as plain as daylight. However it does not mean that Islam has not attached any importance to the things required for the material world. The position assigned to man by Islam as well as the purpose of his creation defined by it refute any idea of this nature. The concept of spiritual attainment and the struggle of a Muslim to achieve the nearness of Allah and the path which Islam has laid down for the realisation of this cherished goal also falsify such a notion. If in spite of these facts someone thinks otherwise he is but ignorant of Islam. "Muslim" or "believer" is not the name of a mere soul but a combination of body and soul. The fulfilment of his duties in this world, the accomplishment of his mission and the struggle for the pleasure of Allah require his body and its physical faculties. Obviously he also needs some material for maintaining them, which we call the economic needs of man. The Prophet *s.a.w.* said:

> "Next to obligatory prayers is the obligation of earning an honest living".

For this reason the Qur'an calls it "the riches of Allah", "Things clean", "Blessings of Allah" and "Favours of Allah". In short Islam attaches full importance to the material needs of man and has made abundant provision in its system that no one is deprived of them. This provision is comprehensive and includes the following effective measures:

(i) It is incumbent on every Muslim that he should himself earn his living.

(ii) Earning and spending is subject to certain limitations.

(iii) Moral obligations of the rich to fulfil the needs of the poor.

(iv) Legal obligations of the rich in regard to the poor.

A brief description of each of these measures is given in seriatum below:

(a) It is incumbent for every Muslim that he should himself earn his living:

> "Earning an honest livelihood is an obligation".

No one should become a burden on others for his livelihood and must earn it through his own labour.

No one would eat a food better than one which he took (after acquiring it with a labour of his hand) (*Bukhari*).

(b) Begging is highly condemnable and one who does it without a genuine cause earns an unlawful livelihood and eats a forbidden food.

"Qubaisah, it is all equal that one eats by begging or through ill-gotten property" (*Muslim*).

(i)   All the lawful avenues of earning a livelihood are open to every one. In economic field every body has equal opportunities of struggle. No monopoly of any kind exists. Agriculture, trade, industry, services, in short every source of earring livelihood, is open to all without any discrimination. Everybody is free to choose a profession of his own liking and aptitude. All sources of livelihood, according to Islam, are created for men by Allah:

He it is Who created for you all that is in the earth (2:29).

(ii) All things in the earth and space, in the creation of which man has not subscribed, can be utilised by all in accordance with their needs. The Prophet *s.a.w.* said:

"All Muslims have equal share in three things, namely water, grass and fire" (Hujjat Allah al-Balighah).

Although this tradition mentions only three things but in fact it lays down a principle that all such things which grow naturally, without any human effort, are free for everyone. Another tradition concerning a person who disallows the use of such things makes this point more clear. The Prophet *s.a.w.* said:

"On the Day of Judgement, Allah will say to such a person that today I deprive you of My blessings as you person did deprive men of the benefits of things you did not make" (Hujjat Allah al-Balighah).

In short, the water of the rivers, ponds and springs, grass and wood of the forests, the fruits of such trees as grow wild, unkept birds, fish, animals of the forest, ores, saltmines and other similar things, are reserved for public use. An abandoned land has also a similar position. Any one who wants to cultivate it can do so without any restriction.

"The waste land belongs to Allah and His Messenger and it is meant for you on My behalf" (*Hujjat Allah al-Balighah*).

(iii) If a person acquires, through his labour, possession of a portion of such a thing as is open to common use, he becomes its owner. It cannot be snatched away from him. There is a saying of the Prophet *s.a.w.* in this regard:

"Any one who cultivates a barren land becomes its owner (*Hujjat Allah al-Balighah*).

(iv) After acquiring the ownership of a natural source of livelihood nobody can keep it idle. If a person keeps a piece of land idle and uncultivated, it would revert to its original state: become a common property again. Whoever likes can take into his possession and bring it under the plough:

"The one who keeps the land uncultivated for three years will have no claim over that land" (*Hujjat Allah al-Balighah*).

(v) Everyone is free to utilise his wealth for multiplying it further. Islam has provided great incentive for its followers for entering the trade and industry, the two major practical sources for multiplying wealth. Great blessings are promised for them who enter those two fields.

(vi) The freedom to multiply wealth is, of course, not absolutely unrestrained. It is subject to certain heavy moral and legal restrictions. These are as follows:

(a) Scrupulous honesty and truthfulness are but essential for every deal. Any contrivance to involve a customer in an unfair deal is a major sin. The Prophet *s.a.w.* said:

"He who deceives is not one of my people".

(b)   Taking of false oaths for the purpose of increasing sales is also a great sin. According to a tradition one who increases his trade by false oaths, would be deprived of the grace of Allah on the Day of Judgement" (*Muslim*).

(c)   Business involving usury in any form is forbidden. Its receipt and payment both are unlawful:

Allah permitteth trading and forbiddeth usury (2:275).

Not only this, it is also a criminal offence of the level of treason. It is declaring war against the Islamic State:

O ye who believe! Fear Allah and relinquish what remains of interest, if you are believers. But if you do it not, then be warned of war (against you) from Allah and His Messenger (2:278-279).

(d)   No such partnership is permissible in which profit of one partner is guaranteed but of the others is not. All such transactions fall in the category of usury.

(e)   Gambling is an unlawful and an impious act.

O ye who believe! Strong drink and games of chance and idols and driving arrows are only an infamy of Satan's handiwork (5:90).

Islam not only forbids ordinary gambling but also such business which is akin to gambling i.e., speculation, lottery, life insurance, etc., etc.

(f)   Trade of all such things is also forbidden which have been held unlawful for eating and drinking:

"Allah and His Prophet has forbidden the trade of liquor, which dies of itself, swine and idols" (*Bukhari*). To speak of their trade even their price is unlawful:

"When Allah forbade to eat a thing, He also forbade its price.

(g) In business such methods which harm others, or the society as a whole, are also not permissible:

   (i) Hoarding of necessities of life, with the motive of selling them afterwards at a higher price, is strictly prohibited. Those who do so have been strongly condemned:

   "Hoarder is accursed" (*Baihaqi*).

   (ii) Buying a merchandise on its way to marketplace is also not permissible.

   "The merchandise flowing towards the market, must not be blocked" (*Muslim*).

   (iii) No one living in a city is allowed to become an agent of a villager who has brought his merchandise for sale in the market. Nor is he allowed to stock his merchandise for the purpose of selling it at a higher price.

   "No citizen should sell the goods of an absentee villager" (*Muslim*).

(h) No such business transaction is permissible in which the merchandise offered for sale is not in the seller's own possession. This is so because such a deal is likely to give rise to disputes. It also, in the long run, assumes the character of speculation, which culminates in the rise of prices.

"Do not sell the merchandise which is not in your possession" (*Abu Dawud*).

(i) All such sources of livelihood which cause material loss to others are forbidden in Islam. Similarly, sources which affect the morality and religion of the public are also unlawful. Intoxicants, dance, music, paintings, obscene literature, cinema (as it is being used at present) and similar things are prohibited as means of livelihood.

(j)   Any business transaction, the complete details of which are not
      clear, and on that account is open to dispute, is also not valid.

      "Allah's Messenger *s.a.w.* has prohibited a fraudulent and
      ambiguous transaction" (*Muslim*).

7.   The wealth earned within the limits stated above is a lawful property and can be spent freely. But, nevertheless, this freedom of
spending is not unlimited. It is also subject to certain moral and legal
limits. One who violates them will be brought to book by the
Government. If, somehow, one escapes its punishment in this world
he would not escape it in the Hereafter. The detail in regard to some
of these restrictions is given in the forthcoming discussion and has
been partly covered in the previous chapter under the title 'Social
System'. The essence of these restrictions is that while there is no bar
on loading a reasonably comfortable and prosperous life, it is
forbidden to live in a luxurious, extravagant, pompous, ostentatious
manner.

Injunctions to the Rich in Respect of
Providing Needs of the Poor

Everyone is equally free to earn and amass wealth. But as all are not
by birth endowed with an equal measure of physical and mental capa-
cities, and conditions and circumstances do not favour everybody
alike, the result of their economic struggle cannot be similar. It is just
the opposite. What actually happens is that while a segment of
society becomes excessively rich there also emerges a section of
society which does not get enough for subsistence even. This
situation obtains in spite of the admitted fact that the provision of the
essentials of life is not only a civil obligation but a religious one also.
Islam regards mankind as "the children of Allah" (*Mishkat*). Since we
do not like to see our children deprived of food and clothing, how
can it be possible that Allah Who is "The Kind" and "The Compass-
ionate", would allow any of His children to live in that plight. For
these reasons Islam stresses that the needs of those who do not

succeed in their economic struggle should be fulfilled by those who have succeeded in it. It is a joint responsibility of both the government and the rich, that they are not left to their misery. The sources of livelihood which Allah has created in this world are meant for all. If for certain reasons some people cannot get enough for their needs from their employment, while others earn more than they need, the excess earning of the latter is not meant for themselves. It is, in fact, the right of others which has passed to them. Such surplus earnings are like the securities of which they are the keepers only. It is their duty that they return them to their rightful owners. While enumerate the qualities of the believers the Qur'an expressly mentions:

And in their wealth the beggar and the outcast had due share (51:19).

Specific jurisdictions are imparted to the rich for paying this right to the poor and the needy. Some of them are given below:

1. *Ye will not attain to piety until ye spend of that which ye love* (3:95).

2. "It is contrary to the faith that a Muslim should sleep well-fed while his neighbour tosses about in his bed tormented by hunger" (*Mishkat*).

3. Richness is a great trial. It is, in fact a great ordeal, which very often leads to a catastrophe. Only those escape its consequences who spend their wealth most willingly on religious affairs and on the needs of the poor. The Prophet *s.a.w.* once said:

"I swear by the Lord of Ka'bah that they will be the losers".

On being asked as to whom he was referring he replied:

"The rich of them. Only those will escape the evil consequences who go on spending their wealth unhesitatingly in the way of Allah and the number of such persons is not large".

Legal Responsibilities of the Rich In respect to the Poor

In consideration of this right of the poor Islam imposed upon the rich certain legal responsibilities over and above the moral ones. These are the following:

1. Everyone, except the poor, has to pay annually to the poor a certain portion of his wealth and produce by way of their legal right. The government recovers the Zakat (poor-due) and the tithe from every member of the society and makes arrangement for its distribution among the poor. No one can refuse it. If anyone does, he not only spoils his After-life but is awarded the severest punishment by the government for his default.

2. If the amount recovered as tithe and Zakat (poor-due) does not suffice for the needs of the poor and other religious requirements, the government has right to levy additional tax on the rich.

3. When a Muslim dies his property is distributed among his nearest relatives. If such close relatives, as are entitled to the property of the deceased, do not exist it goes to other relatives who have a distant relationship with him. (For this purpose, Islam has provided a comprehensive law of inheritance for its followers.) By means of this system the wealth does not concentrate in the hands of a few and goes on spreading in different directions. This system also helps to curtail poverty as it stimulates the circulation of wealth and evolves its appropriate distribution. These two are the best methods for reducing the economic disparity in a society.

5. POLITICAL SYSTEM

   The political system of Islam is based on two basic realities:

   (i) *The personal position of Allah* vis-a-vis this universe, particularly men. He is not only their Creator and Supporter but also their real Master.

(ii) *The personal position of man.* He is not only created and supported by Allah (the Supporter of all the worlds) but is also His humble slave and His vicegerent in this world.

The political system which Islam has constructed over these two basic realities has the following salient features:

1. The supreme authority and sovereignty actually rest with Allah alone. No individual, clan, community or even the whole mankind has an iota of share in it. Man is by birth His slave.

    The decision rests with Allah only, Who hath commanded you that you worship none save Him (12:40).

2. Allah alone is the real Legislator. The constitution given by Him is the constitution of man's life. It alone governs the life of man. No individual or institution has the Power to make one for himself or others.

3. The Prophet of Allah *s.a.w.* is the representative and the expounder if His injunctions and pleasures. By virtue of this position he acquires the status of a subordinate legislator and therefore his orders call for the same obedience that is due to the original Legislator.

    And whatsoever the Messenger giveth you, take it. And whatever he forbiddeth, abstain (from it) (59:7).

    The obedience of the Messenger is nothing but the obedience of Allah:

    Whoso obeyeth the Messenger obeyeth Allah (4:80).

4. For the exact implementation of the Divine injunctions, the setting up of a collective system and a governing institution is but indispensable.

    "The installation of Imam is obligatory here is a consensus of opinion over it". (*Sharah 'Aqaid-i-Nasfiah*, p. 110).

In technical terms it is known as 'Khilafat' or 'Imamat' or 'Amarat'. This institution is comprised of one man who is called 'the Khalifah' or 'the Imam' or 'the Amir'.

5. Everyone who professes faith in Islam is a citizen of the Islamic State. This provision not only includes such Muslims who are born in that state but every Muslim, to whatever country he belongs, becomes its citizen when he enters it.

    And the believers, men and women are protecting friends one of another (9:71).

6. Non-Muslims cannot become the real citizens of an Islamic State. Their position is but of the second-rate citizens. In technical terms they are called "the Zimmis". This is so because an Islamic State is responsible for their life, property and honour. Their rights do not depend on the pleasure of the state or the Khalifah but have been pre-determined by Allah and His Messenger *s.a.w.* and an Islamic State is duty-bound to fulfil them.

7. It is the duty of the Khalifah to run the affairs of the state in accordance with the Divine injunctions, maintain justice among the citizens of the state, defend the state and the nation and above all fulfil the mission of Islam. Allah has bestowed upon them, sent the Prophet Muhammad *s.a.w.* and constituted the Muslim community. In respect of these duties he is answerable to Allah as well as the Muslims.

8. There is a council of advisors to assist the Khalifah in his heavy responsibilities. It is incumbent on him to run the affairs of the state in accordance with their advice. Allah ordained the Prophet *s.a.w.* to seek the advice of his companions in all important matters:

    And consult with them upon the conduct of affairs (3:159)

9. Such a person is appointed as Khalifah whom the Islamic soc-

iety considers most suitable for this heavy responsibility and whose appointment is accepted by the overwhelming majority of the people. He comes into power through election and can be dismissed from his office if he fails to do his duty. If his negligence is aggravated and he deviates from the fundamental principles of Khilafah, it becomes the duty of the Islamic Society to dislodge him from the office.

10. Islam has not specified any method for the election of the Khalifah. All it has done in this field is that on the one hand it has defined the purpose of his election and on the other given guiding principles for doing so. Any system of election which is consonant with these two requirements, the purpose and the guiding principle for election, would be an Islamic System. The purpose is that such a person is elected who is better than the others in knowledge, fear of Allah, sagacity, talents and practical capabilities and who commands the respect of the people and is trusted by them. The guiding principle is that he is elected by such persons who hold a distinguished position by virtue of their intelligence, love of religion and power or decision. The public at large concurs their decision. The guiding principle is provided for a better attainment of the purpose of election.

11. The office of the Khilafah, or for that matter any office of the government, cannot be given to a person who himself desires or demands it:

"By Allah, we will not confer the office upon one who demands it or is covetous about it" (*Bukhari*).

This is so because the Islamic concept of government is different from the ordinary It is a responsibility and security rather than a right, and one would be answerable to Allah for it.

"This (covetousness) for Imamat will be source of disgrace and humiliation except in case of the one who holds it with justification and justifies its holding" (*Muslim*).

For this reason no sensitive Muslim ever ventures to aspire for it. On the Day of Judgement, when he will be presented before Allah, he shall be liable to answer for the rights of the people for whom he was made responsible in this world. The Prophet (peace he upon him) once said:

"In this connection the best among people is one who detests (this office) most" (*Muslim*).

If a Muslim attempts to secure an office while he is ignorant of the responsibilities attached to it, how can you expect him to perform his duty properly. He is not even aware of them.

12.   It is not lawful for anybody to deny the Khilafat of one who is duly elected for this office. One who does so treads not the path of Islam but of ignorance.

"Who dies in a state without a pledge of obedience to Imam, he dies the death of ignorance" (*Muslim*).

His refusal to acknowledge an elected Khalifah is in fact disobedience of the entire Islamic State and a declaration of war against it.

13.   It is the bounden duty of every citizen to obey the orders of the Khalifah:

Obey Allah, and obey the Messenger and those of you who are in authority (4:59).

Disobedience of his orders is virtually the disobedience of Allah and His Messenger *s.a.w.*:

"Whosoever disobeys the Amir, he disobeys me" (*Muslim*)

But if the Khalifah orders something sinful then disobedience of his orders is an obligation:

"If the Amir orders for the disobedience of Allah, then one should neither listen to him or obey him" (*Muslim*).

One is not only required to submit to the authority of the Khalifah but has to wish him well wholeheartedly as well. It is a duty, a constituent of Islam and a characteristic of piety.

"Allah's Messenger said: *Din* is another name of devotion. We said: To whom? Thereupon he said: To Allah, His Messenger and the ruler of the Muslims" (*Muslim*).

14. It is a right, rather a responsibility of every Muslim to keep strict vigilance over the Khalifah and his subordinates. They are to be checked whenever they err. If they follow a wrong cause, they are to be made to pursue the right one. When Abu Bakr (*r.a.*) was elected the Khalifah, he reminded the people of this right of theirs and strongly emphasised the need for making the Khalifah answerable.

"Set me on the right, if I go astray" (*Tabari*).

15. Laws are framed for all such matters in respect or which express Divine injunctions are not available. These laws are made by the Khalifah and his advisory council.

16. The Islamic State is responsible for the life, property and honour of every citizen regardless of his religion. Similarly every citizen is free to practise his religion and enjoys complete freedom of conscience. This freedom is, however, subject to the restriction that no one is allowed to incite people to revolt against the State. Nor has anyone the liberty to say thins which lead to disruption and disorder in the society or cause a moral decline. No one is to be deprived of his freedom without a proper trial of the charge levelled against him.

17. The aim of the establishment of an Islamic State and the responsibility of its government are very noble and vast. The following verses of the Qur'an determine its basic principles:

Verily, we sent our Messengers with clear proofs and revealed with them the Scripture and the Balance, that mankind may observe right measure, and He revealed iron (57:25).

O David, Lo! We have set thee as a vicegerent in the earth, therefore judge aright between mankind (38:27).

Those who, if We give them power in the land, establish worship and pay the poor-due and enjoin kindness and forbid iniquity (22:41).

The first two verses in general and the third one in particular make the purpose of the establishment of the Islamic State clear. The former two verses are indicative of the fact that the function of the government is to establish justice in the society. This is the purpose which all governments strive to attain, or at least claim as their cherished goal. This is the object which makes the existence of a government indispensable. The third verse adds further to this general purpose of the government. It spells out that the real object of the Islamic State is to form a society which establishes the prescribed prayer, pays the Zakat (poor-due), embraces piety and inclines people to virtue, resents what is forbidden in religion and also dissuades others from it. This is the purpose an Islamic State is devoted to and which gives a distinguishing character to it. It is not to be found anywhere else. Not even by way of window-dressing. This object has four principal features i.e., prayer, Zakat, affirmation of the good and the negation of the evil deeds. A careful examination would reveal that it is in fact synonymous with establishing the religion in full measure, making a ceaseless endeavour for enlarging the sphere of religious beneficence and waging an untiring struggle to give a true Islamic colour to the Society.

6.   LEGAL SYSTEM

Following are the basic principles of the Islamic Legal System:
1.   The two principal sources from whence Islamic Law has been drawn are (i) The Qur'an (ii) The Tradition. All such laws which are clearly stated in them are eternal and unchangeable. They are valid for all times and their obedience is but essential.

Even the slightest change is not possible in them. Neither a Khalifah has the authority to make a departure from them for the affairs of the state nor any ruler has the power to deviate from them. Anyone who does so forsakes his religion:

Whoso judgeth not by that which Allah hath revealed: such are the disbelievers (5:44).

2. Laws are framed in respect of questions for which express injunctions are not found in the Qur'an and the Traditions.

These laws are framed in the context of the prevalent circumstances and needs of the times. Only those persons are entrusted with this task as are most competent to do it. Their competence is founded on their knowledge, piety, deep insight in religion, proficiency in legal matters and understanding of the needs of the times. It is not just a routine legislation simply because it concerns only such matters for which express injunctions are not given in the Qur'an and the Tradition. Such a legislation is neither unlimited nor independent. It is subject to the temperament of religion and the prescribed objections of the Islamic system (Shari'ah). The legislators keep in constant view the injunctions of the Qur'an and the Traditions. These injunctions are in fact the bed-rock of their legislation.

This process of legislation is technically known as "*Qiyas*". The nature of the laws so framed is different from the Divine laws. While the Divine laws are absolute, unchangeable and everlasting, the laws framed by men are not. There can be a difference of opinion in regard to them and they are also liable to change. It is so because these laws are the outcome of the opinion and intelligence of men in which difference can arise. They are open to change because they are framed in the context of the prevalent circumstances and needs of time which are ever changing. Such a law is, however, an exception which is endorsed by the overwhelming majority of technical experts. It acquires the position of the absolute law. This consensus of experts is technically known as "Ijma".

Thus there are four sources of Islamic law, namely, the Qur'an,
the *Sunnah* (the Traditions), the *Qiyas* and the *Ijma*.

3. The judiciary is completely independent of the Executive. Any
    control or influence of the executive over the legislation is out
    of question. The law-makers are entrusted with the responsibility
    of interpreting the Divine laws to the best of their ability. While
    doing his duty the only principle that a legislator bears in mind
    is that he deals with the question referred to him in the manner
    in which, according to his own assessment, it would have been
    dealt with by Allah, if it was presented before Him.

4. Like the judiciary, the Executive is also completely independent.
    The appointment of the *Qazi* or the Judges is also made, directly
    or indirectly, by the Government. But when a *Qazi* or Judge is
    appointed, he is not a subordinate of the Government but of
    Allah. The only thing he then has a regard for is the Islamic
    Law and nothing else.

5. The authority of the law is invincible. No one is above the law.
    The distinction of the rich and the poor, the commanded and the
    privileged classes ceases to exist. Even the highest in the
    society, not excepting even the Khalifah, is as much subordinate
    to law as a helpless beggar. If the Khalifah, is required by the
    court in any case, he would appear before it in the same way as
    others do. Similarly, if he is held guilty in any case by the Court
    he shall have to undergo the punishment awarded to him. These
    words of the Prophet *s.a.w.* stand unparalleled in the history of
    the Judiciary:

    "Even if Fatimah, the daughter of Muhammad had committed a
    theft, I swear by Allah, I would have cut off her hands"
    (*Bukhari*).

The Khalifah does not have the power to stop the enforcement of
punishment for such sins as have been expressly stated in the Qur'an
and the Traditions. If theft is committed the hands of the thief shall

be chopped off. One who commits adultery shall be scourged with stripes, or stoned to death. One who makes a baseless accusation of adultery against someone shall have to bear eighty stripes. The murderer, who has not been forgiven by the heirs of the victim shall be executed. In an Islamic State, a Governor or Head of the State is not empowered to hear an appeal of mercy in such cases.

6. Punishments for criminal offences are enforced in normal conditions only. As long as the society does not acquire the true Islamic character, or the conditions remain abnormal and the people commit crimes out of sheer despair, these punishments will not be enforced. The punishment of theft was once suspended in the reign of Khalifah 'Umar (*r.a.*) when the state was in the grip of an acute famine.

7. Justice will be dispensed to everyone. There is no such thing as 'Court Fee' which is recovered by way of payment for the dispensation of justice.

12

RELIGION AND POLITICS
AN IMPORTANT PROBLEM OF OUR TIMES

It has been made clear in the previous chapters that Islam has a comprehensive system of life of which political system constitutes a part. How politics is a part of religion and how political system is constituent of the religious system is a point which is not yet abundantly clear. What is its significance and importance? It seems necessary that this point should be dealt with at some length. Politics is not something which can be ignored as a trivial affair. In the present-day world its importance has increased so much that even the most personal affairs are not outside its scope. It is, therefore, natural that it should have a far-reaching effect on man's life. Any one with a pair of eyes can see that all the philosophies, ideals and beliefs are swept away by the tide of politics. On the other hand it is contended that politics should have nothing to do with religion. Illusive arguments are advanced in support of this contention. It is argued that since religion is a medium of man's access to God, something highly sacred and sublime, it is unfair to drag it in the worldly affairs. What is sacred should be kept in sacred places. This concept is in vogue more or less in the whole world. Not to speak of anything more, people are not even inclined to accept that religion can have any kind of link with politics.

This discussion could be altogether ignored and we could proceed further without touching upon this controversy if this misconception had not extended to the followers of Islam also. The present situation is such that many of those who are not Muslims for name's sake only but are the true followers of Islam, and claim to see Islam independent of others' views, say that its; relation with politics is not crucial. In their opinion its importance in religion is not basic but secondary. Not to speak of indispensibiliy it is not even required in Islam. They think that it is not an incumbent religious duty of a Muslim to strive for the establishment of an Islamic State. They consider it a Divine prize which is given to those by Allah who follow the religion sincerely. In short, if Islamic State is required, it is not for Islam but for its followers.

What link Islam has with politics is a question that has gained extraordinary importance in modern times due to the reasons just stated. If politics is a constituent of Islam, what is its significance and importance? It is a question which calls for an elaborate discussion and straight-forward answer. It would not be possible to understand Islam properly if this question is left unanswered. The picture of Islam which would emerge without it would be blurred.

The importance of this issue warrants that all its aspects should be kept in view and all such factors which can help us in determining the true relationship of religion with politics be examined in their proper sequence.

Belief and the Concept of Politics

For the purpose in view we should first of all see the attributes of Allah, because they are in fact the fountain-head whence all religious concepts and Divine injunctions emerge. It is therefore, the prerogative of these attributes to decide as to what relation religion has with politics.

In the second chapter of this book (entitled "Fundamental Beliefs) we have already studied in detail that Sovereignty is one of the basic attributes of Allah. Some verses which provide evidence to this effect are as under:

Say! I take refuge in the Lord of mankind, the King of mankind, the God of mankind (114:1-3).

Verily, His is all creation and commandment (7:54),

Ye worship none save Him (12:40).

These verses reveal that Allah is not only the Lord and God of Mankind but also their King and Ruler. He is such a Lord God whose Lordship and Godliood include Kingship, Autocracy and Mastery. It clearly means that the real King and Ruler and the Law-Giver is Allah and being so is one of His undisputed and important attributes. Until and unless one has implicit faith in these attributes, he cannot be accepted as a believer.

When it is an accepted fact that the King, the Ruler and the Law-Giver is none but Allah, it is in other words an advice that the political life of man should be constructed over the unshared Supremacy of Allah. This is because the primary question of politics and its fundamental clause relates to the supremacy of power and determination of supreme authority. The attributes of Kingship of Allah provide the correct answer of it.

Islamic Law and Politics

After studying the attributes of Allah let us now examine the complete code of Islamic Law. Generally the following issues come in the purview of politics and form the matrix of man's political life.

Why a collective social order is necessary? In whom does the society vest the supreme authority? What is the real status of man? What are the basic rights of an individual? What are the powers of government and what is their extent? Who frames the constitution? What type of constitution is in force? Let us see whether these questions have been discussed in the Qur'an and the Tradition and their answers are included in them? An answer to this question has already been given in the chapter entitled "Political System of Islam." It has been made clear in that chapter that Islam has taken up all the questions which lie in the scope of politics and has prescribed injunctions in respect of each of them. It means that Islam has a complete political system of life.

Adherence to Religion and the Authority of Government

A very large number of Islamic injunctions included in the Islamic Law are such that their enforcement without a political system and an authoritative government is not possible. For instance:

1. If anyone commits a murder, it is obligatory for the heirs of the victim to retaliate.

    O ye who believe! retaliation is prescribed for you in the matter (2:178).

2. The Qur'an enjoins to chop off the hands of the thief.

    As for the thief, both male and female, chop off their hands (5:38).

3. One who is guilty of adultery is to be punished with a hundred stripes.

    The adulterer and the adultness, scourge ye each one of them with a hundred stripes (24:2).

4. One who makes a false accusation of adultery against someone is liable to a punishment of eighty stripes.

    And those who accuse honourable woman but bring not four witnesses, scourge them (with eighty stripes) (24:4).

5. The Qur'an enjoins war against the enemies of Islam and orders to crush them completely.

    And fight them until persecution is no more, and religion is for Allah (2:139).

Similarly there are many other injunctions of this kind which cannot be implemented, adequately without a government. Such injunctions can only be practised properly if an organised government exists. For instance, take, the case of the following injunctions:

1. The Muslims are enjoined to crush the hypocrites with iron

hands:

"Whosoever among you sees evil, let him check that with his hand" (*Bukhari*).

2. The Qur'an advises the believers to remain firm on the path of justice:

    Be ye staunch in justice, witnesses for Allah (4:135).

3. The temporal courts are not worthy of it that the Muslims take their matters for adjudication to them:

    How they go for judgement (in their disputes) to false deities when they have been ordered to abjure them (4:60)

4. Public disputes should be adjudicated in accordance with the Divine Law:

    So judge between them by that which Allah hath revealed (5:48).

5. The very purpose of the creation of the Muslim is that they should verify the truthfulness of the Divine religion before the whole mankind:

    That Ye may be a witness against mankind (2:143).

Obviously the compliance of such religious injunctions is as important as of the others, because they are as much constituents of the religious laws as the others are. Their compliance is a religious obligation in the same manner as of the others as Allah has not given us the discretion to discriminate in His injunctions. We do not have the liberty to act upon what we like and leave what we do not. Allah commands us to comply with all of His injunctions without discrimination.

Follow that which is sent down unto you from your Lord (7:3).

If we do not do so and exercise discrimination, and choice of the compliance of Divine injunctions this practice would not be in keeping with belief but disbelief. The example of the Jews is before us who were held guilty of such a defalcation:

Believe ye in part of the Scripture and disbelieve ye in part thereof (2:85).

Politics is an Integral Part of the Religion

Let us now consider all these things collectively as it would completely solve the question of the relationship of Islam and Politics.

If sovereignty is one of the basic attributes of Allah, and it implies that the political life of man should be based on the belief in His unshared Sovereignty, then it is a proof of the fact that man's political life lies within the orbit of religion. It cannot be excluded from it. If we regard it otherwise the relief in the Sovereignty will become void. If a part of the "Divine Law consists of its political canons, and if Islam contains a full-fledged political. order as well, it amply proves that any concept wherein a political system is wanting would be at variance with the true and complete concept of Islam. Actually we cannot even imagine a true and complete Islam which lacks a political system. It is as if you wish to imagine a physically perfect and healthy person you would not be able to get along by imagining his organs and limbs in isolation. You would have to imagine him as a whole.

It is established in the above discussion that in the absence of a sovereign power a very large number of religious injunctions cannot be implemented while, as we very well know, the negligence of any constituent of Islam is most sinful and un-Islamic act. Does it not clearly mean that politics is but an integral part of Islam? Politics is not only important in its own right, it acquires a tremendous significance when we find that life and vitality of so many Islamic injunctions also depends upon it.

When we see the dimensions of the superb importance of politics in Islam we learn the truth and reality contained in those words of

'Umar, the Great (*r.a.*):

> "There can be no idea of Islam except through a *Jama'at* and
> there can be no idea of *Jama'at* except a through leader."

K'ab al-Ahbar, who is renowned among those who conversed with
the companions of the Prophet Muhammad *s.a.w.* stated this fact in
more elaborate terms when he said:

> "Islam, the government and the masses are likened to a tent and
> its pole and pegs. The tent is Islam pole, the is the government
> and pegs are the masses. None of these can remain in its correct
> position without the other two". (*Al-'Aqdul Farid, Vol.1*)

In short if Islam is detached from the concept of politics and
government what remains is something other than Islam bestowed
upon us by Allah, revealed in the Qur'an and practised by the
Prophet Muhammad *s.a.w.* Islam can only be seen in its true form
if it is placed in a position of complete authority.

Another revolutionary characteristic of Islam is its view of
political power. It does not consider political power a worldly prize
but a religious one. Not a thing to be detested and abstained from but
to be relished and required. Islam is not indifferent to it. Rather
Islam has a strong passion and yearning for it, because until and
unless it is possessed with power it cannot fulfil the purpose of its
existence.

Islamic Government and Muslim Government

Here it seems pertinent to point out the difference between an
"Islamic Government' and a "Muslim Government". Islam is not a
living organism who can attain the required political power through
its own endeavour and retain it by himself. It can actually achieve
power through its followers only. They can achieve it by dint of their
own struggle and once this is done they can manage to retain it.
Therefore, the true followers of Islam are those who have the reigns
of government in their hands or who constantly strive to attain it.

There is, however, a world of difference in their motive for gaining political power. It can be for their own supremacy and for the glory of Islam. The power of the first kind would be 'Muslim power' and the second would be designated 'Islamic power'. In Divine judgement the former is temporal and the latter 'religious'. While the first one is evil, the second one is good. One plays havoc with the world, the other embellishes it. This is why the Qur'an has made it a standard of judgement for its believers. On the one hand it has defined the believers as:

Those who seek not oppression in the earth, nor yet corruption (28:83).

On the other hand the Qur'an addresses the believers and gives them good tidings in these words:

Ye shall overcome them if ye are (indeed) believers. (3:139).

It means that power and domination which is for one's private gain is in fact nothing but oppression and revolt. It crams the world with evils and a devout believer cannot even think of it. But such exaltation and power which is meant for the service of Islam are good and virtuous and a Muslim inwardly craves for it. There can hardly be any doubt about it that in essence the two types of political powers are quite different from one another. They are as different in their basic concepts as they are in their consequences. In appearance both are political powers and both are for the Muslims, but while the one is in the nature of a sacred trust and responsibility, the other is for personal ends. People who look at things superficially can be deceived by them but such a vast and fundamental difference between the two cannot escape those who are endowed with insight and understanding. They will feel that although both the birds fly through the same air still the world of the falcon and the vulture is not the same.

Mission of the Prophets and the Power to Rule

The nature, the importance and the need for close relationship between politics and religion, discussed in the above paragraphs, reveal a truth of superb importance. The truth that the mission assigned to the Prophets was in the last analysis practically nothing but the establishment of a religious and Islamic government. It has been so because without the ruling power Divine religion cannot be practised to its full extent. This contention was as much true in the times of those Prophets as it is today in the case of Islam. It was, therefore. because of this imperative need that the Divine religions devoted all their energies to acquire the reins of government. It is a different matter that the prevailing circumstances were not favourable to many of them and their struggle did not yield the best results. Obviously, a mission's inability to attain the zenith of success is one thing and its inner perfection another. No doubt the history of the Prophet's mission shows that many of them could not establish a political order of their own but there is no evidence to show that they did not even want to do so. It is true that the basis of the invitation of each Prophet was "There is no god except Allah" and not "There is no sovereign except Allah" but nevertheless it is equally true that meanings of "There is no god except Allah" also include "There is no sovereign except Allah," as sovereignty is one of the basic attributes of Allah. It means that when it is said that "There is no god except Allah" it also means "There is no sovereign except Allah" It is certainly wrong to regard Allah as Sovereign only. But it is far more wrong to exclude the attributes of Sovereignty from the concept of Allah. It would be true to say that none of the Prophets gave his invitation in the words:

> "Ye mankind! establish the sovereignty of Allah as you have no sovereign except Him"

Instead of these words every Prophet actually said:

> *Serve Allah. Ye have no other god save Him* (7:59).

But who would contest that the meanings of these words do not also include the sense and significance of the preceding quotation. This could only be done if the meaning of the words worship were confined to prayer only. But actually it is not so. The word worship signifies both worship as well as submission. As such the compliance of religious injunctions which relate to the various aspects of life, and of which the last link is politics and government cannot be excluded from worship. If the compliance of these injunctions is also worship then the actual mission of each Prophet also precluded the compliance of the Divine political injunctions.

It may be asked here that in the mission of the Prophets introduced in the Qur'an there is no mention of political injunctions anywhere. Their missions consisted of beliefs, ethics and worship of one singular God (Allah) only. The injunction " worship Allah" seems to be limited to prayer only because when some Prophets proclaimed "There is no god except Allah" and ordained "worship Allah" and illustrated their saying with their words and deeds, then their statement and action should be treated as a standard explanation of these terms. If the meanings of these words included politics as well there must have been a mention of it somewhere. If they had not imparted political injunctions to their followers they could at least show them that the establishment of the Divine Government was their final aim. In short, if politics was a primary constituent of the religion of every Prophet why did they not give such an explanation of the words "worship Allah" as it would have made the position of politics in the religion abundantly clear.

But this question arises if we lose sight of the two cardinal principles of Divine laws. Firstly, no constituent of the Islamic Law is revealed before its scheduled time and practical need. Allah imparts His Divine injunctions when they are necessitated by the affairs of a society and when its people are in a position to act upon them. It is an established principle of the Divine law and its need and expediency are evident. Secondly, it would be wrong to assume that on the basis of this principle such Divine injunctions which are revealed at a subsequent stage are of secondary importance. Similarly, if, in accordance with this principle, religious laws in respect of certain affairs of life are not revealed, it does not mean that they were unimportant and for that reason could not be made a part of the Divine law.

These principles would be better explained by the following examples:

In the words of the Prophet Muhammad *s.a.w.* "war in the cause of Allah (*Jihad*) is the highest peak of Islam" and "best of the acts." But before the second year of Hijrah (Islamic calendar) it was not only regarded so but prohibited. Why was it so? Because the conditions and circumstances required for such a war had not yet arisen. Similarly, usury is the worst kind of sins. It is described as a "revolt against Allah and His Prophet,"and one who indulges in usury is punishable like the disbelievers in the After-life. But it was declared unlawful on the later stage, in the 9th year of the Islamic calendar. Prior to it usury was permitted. Reason being that before that time the society was not in a position to implement it. Had it been enforced earlier it would have upset the whole economic system. Same is the case of liquor. In spite of the fact that it is considered as the mother of all the evils, it was not declared unlawful till the revelation of Surah Maidah (Table) of the Qur'an. The examples cited above are sufficient to vindicate the principles of the Divine law under discussion.

If these two principles are kept in view all the riddles of the question would be automatically resolved. If Allah did not reveal political injunctions to some of the Prophets and did not ordain them and their followers to establish Divine rule the reason was not that such injunctions were unimportant and could not constitute a part of the Divine law framed for them but the actual reason was that a situation had not emerged in which any talk in respect of politics and government would have been relevant. All of us know that certain things are indispensable for the establishment of a system and politics. For instance a reasonable number of people, social system and unity and an independent environment. If the mission of a Prophet did not attain a stare where all these things were present, how and why he and his followers could be given political injunctions. In the mansion of the Divine law the position of these injunctions is that of the plaster of the roof. Until and unless the foundations are laid, the walls raised and the roof constructed, the order for plastering the roof cannot be given. Nor any step can be taken in this direction. Before the completion of these requirements, if the order for plastering the roof is not given and no step taken in this direction, does it prove that the original plan of the house had an unplastered roof? Obviously, it is foolish to think so. Every sane person would think that the plastering of the roof is included in the design of the roof but as a stage has not yet arrived when anything could be said or done about it, so nothing was done about it. If that stage had arrived, the plaster would also be made ready. Similar was the condition of the mission of the Prophets. Such missions which were disrupted before attaining the stage where political injunction would become indispensable, did not include any element of politics and government. As such their followers were absolved of the duty of establishing the rule of Allah which is implied in the Divine injunction, "worship Allah.". It does not mean that the establishment of government in its own right did not deserve to be included in this injunction. Certainly it did. But it was not included because of the prevailing circumstances. Such missions which attained that stage were given political injunctions without least delay. The establishment of a system of government and enforcement of political laws were then also incorporated in the injunction enjoining "worship Allah," in the same manner as were the other constituents of religion. Ever since the establishment of Divine Government and compliance of political laws were made as obligatory at the compliance of any other religious injunction.

Invitation to Islam and the Government

The whole world knows that Islam was one of such mission as succeeded in attaining that stage. This is why its religious law also contains in detail the principles of politics and government. The Prophet of Islam, Muhammad *s.a.w.* not only attained power and laid down a regular system of government, he also headed it. His best companions also maintained this system as a religious duty of vital importance and headed it. Therefore as far as Islam is concerned it cannot be said that the establishment of Divine rule is excluded frcm the original injunction "worship Allah" and politics is net a part of religion. This is one of the numerous reasons why Islam gained the distinction of being a real and all-round perfect religion. While enumerating the degrees of Divine religion, Shah Waliullah says:

"Let it be known that the most perfect religious law and complete Divine guidance is that which enjoins war in the cause of Allah" (*Hujjat Allah al-Balighah*).

"Which enjoins war in the cause of Allah" means that such religious law which includes injunctions in respect of government and politics because war in the cause of Allah is not possible without a regular government.

Islam is not only such a Divine Law which enjoins war in the cause of Allah, it is in fact the one which has regarded it as a standard of religion. Islam is eternal and so its relationship with the war in the cause of Allah. This is an undeniable proof of the fact that the concepts of politics and government cannot be separated from the concept of Islam. If it is separated from Islam what remains is a crippled Islam which would not deserve the distinction of its being a perfect religion mentioned in the Qur'an:

"This day have I perfected your religion for you".

13

ISLAMIC LAW AND WORSHIP

Status of Worship

Religion is in fact but another name of worship of Allah. Its need and significance lies in the fact that it instructs people in Divine worship and in nothing else. It is the submission and worship which purifies and exalts the spirit of man and makes him worthy of His pleasure and blessings. This is the usual conception of religion and it is not an easy matter to refute it. The Qur'an regards it as an open truth. In plain terms it says that the mission of every Prophet was none other than this:

(1) *Serve Allah and shun false gods* (16:30).

This is exactly what the Prophet Muhammad *s.a.w.* also preached when he said:

(2) *O mankind! Worship your Lord* (2:21).

Prophet *s.a.w.* made it explicitly clear by saying that this is the one and only purpose for which man was actually created. Allah has declared in clear-cut terms

(3) *I created the jinn and mankind only that they worship Me* (51:56).

Worship is the objective for which mankind was created and the Prophets were sent to remind it that this alone was the reason of its creation. This is how the two things became linked. The objective of the creation of mankind having been determined, the mission of the Prophets became obvious. It was simply this and nothing else that they keep on reminding mankind of the purpose of its creation.

Meaning of Worship

This status and importance of worship brings to our mind the question of how this worship is related to the exposition of Islam presented in the preceding chapters? In its real sense Islam is a complete system covering every aspect of man's life. It is so comprehensive that it includes everything whether it is belief, worship or any other aspect of man's temporal life. It governs man's whole life. Would it be just to regard the observance of this complete code and every part of it as worship? The limited conception of religion in vogue gives rise to this question.

So far as the practical importance of this is concerned every sensible person would feel that it is but extraordinary. It has a direct and close contact with Islamic law. The answer to this question will have a great bearing on Islamic law. If Islam also has the ordinary conception of worship then those of its elements which relate to the beliefs, worship and attributes of faith deserve greater devotion and fervour than the others. Otherwise, such discrimination would be uncalled for and it will be imperative to consider the observance of entire Islamic law as worship. Every part of it shall have to be observed with equal attention, zeal and fervour. This is what makes the knowledge of the real meanings of worship so important for the right observance of Islam. Its ignorance leads one but astray. In the absence of this knowledge one would concentrate on what he will consider worship and neglect what he will not consider so.

What are the meanings and scope of the word worship when it is mentioned in the Qur'an and the Tradition? In order to grasp its true significance we shall have to examine everything which is of any importance and can be referred to by way of authority for determining the true meanings of this word. This would enable us to do full justice to the understanding of this vital issue and provide us with a reliable answer of our question.

i. *Literal Meanings*

First of all let us turn to the dictionary for the ordinary meanings of this word. Lexicographers say:

(1) "Worship means to lie flat, and absolutely low"

"Worship means degradation of the last degree lying flat" (*Mufradat Imam Raghib*).

(2) "Worship means submission" (*Lisan al-'Arab*).

(3) "He prayed to Allah means he worshipped Allah".

On this analogy "*Abd*" is a slave. "*Tariq-i-Mu'bad*" is a passage which becomes smooth and plain through excess of traffic (*Lisan al-'Arab*).

These meanings of worship may appear different from one another but in fact they are not. There is a close resemblance among them. The real meanings of the word are those which have already been mentioned i.e., to incline, to submit completely, to degrade oneself before someone, to be downtrodden, to lie low. Obviously inclination of the extreme degree acquires the form of complete obedience and as such worship also means submission. If such a being before whom one lays himself and unto whom one degrades himself to the last degree, is possessed of the Divine attributes of mercy and bounty, then his inclination would not be lacking in gratitude. Such inclination, in which this spirit pervades, acquires the form of worship. It is, therefore, but natural, that prayer also means worship.

If we keep the above mentioned explanation in view it will make the Islamic conception of worship a great deal clear. It will also make the essence of worship more intelligible. Who is the worshipper of Allah? If the inclination of the last degree is the basic and real meaning of worship then it logically follows that this is the essence of the worship. As Allah is Sovereign and the real Benefactor of man, it does not stand to reason that his inclination of the last degree to Him would he superficial and not attaining the degree of true submission and worship. It is as unlikely as the idea of burning fire without heat. In short the submission of man unto Allah impels us to believe that it includes all the three things i.e., absolute inclination, submission and worship.

ii.   *Religious Connotation*

The discussion just concluded had a literary aspect. Let us now also examine its religious connotation. It is an established fact that the Prophets came to mankind for its guidance. They enjoined worship of Allah in unambiguous terms. If mankind is created for the worship of Allah, how could the mission of the Prophets be any different? Obviously, this is how it should have been.

When it is a plain fact that the sole mission of the Prophets was to enjoin upon mankind the worship of Allah and to make them His true slaves, it clearly means that whatever they told and taught as Prophets was nothing but His worship.

The Prophets were sent to mankind with the singular mission of enjoining upon them the worship of Allah and to make them His true slaves. Hence whatever they told and taught as Prophets was nothing but His worship. No Prophet ever overstepped the Divine mission entrusted to him. In fact even ordinary persons do not usually back out from tasks assigned to them and Prophets are less likely to commit such an indiscretion. A Prophet is an embodiment of submission. His eyes are fixed all the time on his mission. He imparts to mankind nothing except the Divine message. He does not say a word of his own. Such being his position how can it be possible that in the performance of his duties he would digress and say things not relevant to his mission. It will be, therefore, admitted that whatever a Prophet says is worship without any exception. No matter whether it is fundamental beliefs or the minute social and cultural details. The observance of laws of prayers of Allah is as much a worship as is the compliance of injunctions pertaining to individual and social life. In other words it is the worship enjoining observance of full religion and compliance of the entire Islamic law for which man is created and Prophets have been sent by Allah. The greater the number of Divine injunctions he faithfully follows, the more perfect is his worship. Conversely, the less complete this observance, the more imperfect is his worship.

The basic truths and the universally accepted principles of religion also determine the same meanings of worship in another way. According to the Qur'an the sole purpose of man's Creation is the worship of Allah. It was, therefore, natural for the Qur'an to hold that the first and last position of man was but that of a slave. This is why this fact has been repeated in the Qur'an so often. Let us now see what the true position of a slave is? When a slave is purchased he is a slave of his master for all the twenty-four hours of the day. Whatever he does at his bidding is regarded as service. Now the fact is that the owner of the slave is not his real master. What he has actually purchased is his working capacity and his body and soul. But man is so much a slave and bondsman of Allah that every fibre of his is owned by Him, Everything that the slave has is His and His alone. It is His without any partnership. So far as a true Muslim is concerned he is not only His born slave but His avowed bondsman also. The Qur'an has explained this fact in the following verse:

Lo! Allah hath bought from the believers their lives and their wealth because the Gardens will be theirs (9:3).

As such a Muslim is a slave of Allah not merely in his working capacity, he is His complete slave in all respects. He is His creature as well as His purchased slave. This bargain he has made with his own free will. A Muslim is a born slave who has completely sold himself to Allah. Whatever he does in obedience to his Master cannot be isolated from his servile position. When he is nothing but a slave, each of his acts is bound to be an act of submission. So much so that if the ordinary daily chores are performed by him in accordance with the Divine injunctions, as he must, all such things would be but acts of worship.

The argument put forth in the above paragraph is of deductive nature and has been evolved from certain fundamental religious truths. But the fact is that in spite of its deductive character it comes next to Divine arguments and cannot be challenged for discussion's sake even.

iii.   *The term Worship as used In the Qur'an*

Let us now see how the word worship has been used in the Qur'an. It will be admitted that the true meanings of this word would only be those which have been given to it by the Qur'an. If a survey of the Qur'anic verses can lead us to some conclusions it will be certainly the most authentic and reliable one.

This word has been used in the Qur'an in different forms at numerous places. Some of its usages are examined here in their proper sequence:

(1) *Those whom ye worship beside Him are, but names which ye have named, ye and your fathers* (12:140).

(2) *They said: we worship idols, and are ever devoted to them* (26:71).

These verses indicate that adopting an attitude of worship unto someone amounts this worship. What the infidels did to their idols has been referred here as worship. Obviously the relation of infidels with their idols was but of worship.

(3) *And those who put away false gods lest they should worship them; and turn to Allah in repentance, for them there are glad tidings* (39:17).

(4) *Worse (is the case of him) whom Allah hath cursed, him on whom His wrath hath fallen! Worse is he of whose sort Allah hath turned some to apes and swine, and who serveth idols*

(5:60).

These verses reveal that to consider someone as an absolute sovereign and to obey his injunctions with free will and pleasure is synonymous with his worship. The conduct of those who turn to false gods has been regarded as worship. The Arabic ward used here is *"Taghut"* which literally means "one who exceeds limits or one who becomes a rebel". Technically it means a community which turns its back on the worship of Allah or leads others astray. On this analogy the Satan and the idols are the *Taghuts*. Similar is the case of those rulers, chiefs and national and religious leaders who are devoid of the fear of Allah and indifferent to the Divine injunctions, who elevate their opinion and pleasure to the status of the law of their times. The people who follow these ungodly creatures see no harm in respecting them and consider them worthy of issuing orders and passing judgements. They obey their orders with devotion. If the Qur'an regards such conduct of theirs as 'worship of false gods', it goes to prove that in its opinion an obedience backed by unconditional submission, free will and unqualified consent also amounts to worship.

(1) *And they said : Shall we put faith in two mortals like ourselves, and whose folk are servile unto us* (23:47).

(2) *And this is the past favour wherewith thou reproachest me: that thou hast enslaved the children of Israil* (26:22).

These verses are proof of the fact that not only is such obedience and submission as good as prayer which is backed up by three conditions, namely free will, unqualified consent and uncond- itional submission to the one who is being worshipped, but beyond this such submission is also worship which one may be doing unwillingly, but which is nevertheless done intentionally consciously and unhesitatingly and wherein he who is being worshipped does not consider himself subordinate to any superior power. This is why in the verses cited above the servility of the children of Israil has been called the worship of the Copt (Qibtis). It is but evident that although the children of Israil, being slaves, were utterly helpless and could do nothing to emancipate themselves. They were not putting up with it willingly. It was the terror of the ruling class and their own helplessness which forced them to submit silently to the orders of the oppressors. It shows that unhesitant submission of one who claims to be an absolute monarch is also worship.

(1) *Did I not charge you, O ye sons of Adam, that ye worship not the devil—Lo! he is your open foe* (36 : 60).

(2) *O my father! Serve not the devil* (19:44).

These verses reveal yet another form of worship. They indicate that complete submission of someone is also worship even though it is done unconsciously. This is so because these verses speak of the worship of the devil whereas the true position then obtaining was that the beliefs and practices of the people referred to happened to suit the devil. Otherwise, in point of fact, none of them actually bowed or prayed unto the devil. Nor did anyone accept the devil as his lord or guide. Nor did anyone have any regard for him. In fact they considered him as much an embodiment of evil as did the others and therefore had nothing but hatred and curses for him. But in spite of all this they have been called "the worshippers of devil" in these verses. It clearly means that even if there is no intention of sub-mission, or there is not even a remote idea of imitating someone's precepts and notions, still if through sheer coincidence, there occurs a similarity between the ideal and the follower, even this unconscious submission is held as worship by the Qur'an.

It would not be correct to say that in any of the above mentioned four usages of the Qur'an the word worship has been used metaphorically. Such a statement will be utterly devoid of sense as it would fail to find any support from the dictionary, the Qur'an and the Tradition. Such a claim could only be made if any of the numerous verses of the Qur'an, wherein this word occurs, had indicated that it alone meant worship and nothing else and any act other than that was not so. But there is no verse in the Qur'an which could verify this claim. On the contrary it has many such verses wherein this word has been used for worship (some instances of which have also been cited above). But there is a world of difference in saying that it only means worship that it means worship as well.

If we keep in view the study of the literal meanings of worship we will realize that the four types of worship, which we have come across in these Qur'anic verses, cannot be regarded as four established but mutually unconnected versions of worship. They are in fact four different aspects of the same comprehensive meaning. Worship is submission and conscious or unconscious submission is worship also. Without submission it is just nothing. But neither of it is self-sufficient. If any of these had been so there was no need or justification to regard the others so. But we see that if the Qur'an has regarded worship as submission, it has alongside called the other three forms of submission as worship. It means that in the opinion of the Qur'an submission attains its true meanings only if worship and submission are both combined.

Now we have before us all the three aspects of this study and debate i.e., lexicographical assumptions, the dictates of religious verities and of Qur'anic context. All the three agree that submission is a comprehensive term which covers both submission and worship. Its scope amply covers the religious requirements and Islamic injunctions.

iv. *Submission Required by the Qur'an*

Worship of Allah which is the sole object of man's creation, and which constituted the mission of the Prophets, could not have been something unsettled and raw. It could neither be limited to worship, nor restricted to submission alone. This is what appeals to reason and this is what the Qur'an has also decided. It stands to reason because such a God who is man's Creator, Master, Provider and Benefactor,

Ruler and Object of worship, in short, everything for him, deserves that all kinds of worship should be directed towards Him. It is a decision of the Qur'an in the sense that its verses demand from its followers worship as well submission in equal degree. Its verses exhort the Muslims to bow unto Him only, glorify only His name, address their prayer to Him only, proclaim only His greatness, seek His help only and acknowledge His blessings all the time. These verses at the same time repeatedly enjoin to unconditionally accept Allah as the Ruler and worthy of submission, to accept Him as the Law-Maker, to obey His orders, to adjudicate matters in accordance with His injunctions, to adopt the code prescribed by Him, to consider only that as lawful which, He has declared so and treat only that unlawful which He has forbidden. Therefore the meaning of that worship would only be complete which is the ideal and objective of man's creation and which was the essence of the Prophet's mission. This is what the Qur'an has ordained and in this worship and submission both are included. For further clarification let us consider it from another angle. On one occasion the Qur'an reveals the purpose of man's creation in the following words:

(1) *Who hath created life and death that He may try you in best conduct* (67:2).

On another occasion it is said:

(2) *And when thy Lord said unto angels: Lo! I am about to place a vicegerent on the earth* (2:30).

In revealing the purpose and object of man's creation where the Creator has adopted the term worship, He has used the words best conduct and 'vicegerent' also. It means that although these are separate words but their meanings are not different and have been used only to make the literary expression compatible with different situations. In other words, in the opinion of the Qur'an, the worship of Allah, best conduct and vicegerency are different interpretation of one and the same objective. Therefore any such meanings of worship will not be correct which are not consonant with the concepts of best conduct and vicegerency. Only such meanings of it would be genuine which include the essence of other two as well. Obviously, submission alone cannot be regarded as 'best conduct'. Similar is the case of the 'vicegerency'. Although its apparent meaning are comparatively closer to submission than worship, yet the latter is not outside its meanings. Thus these two interpretations make it evident that Islamic concept of worship covers both worship as well as submission, and no religious, matter is outside its orbit.

It was unlikely that such a fact escaped the attention of the competent religious scholars. When Imam Ibn Taimiya was asked the meanings and significance of the verse: *O mankind! worship your Lord* (2:21). in which worship has been ordained, he spoke at length on this issue and observed:

"Worship is a comprehensive word. It includes all the open and secret acts and teachings which are, liked by Allah and which are the means of winning His pleasure. For instance the prescribed prayer, fast, pilgrimage, truthfulness, integrity, kindness, honesty, obedience of parents, fulfilment of promise, preaching of virtue and fighting the evil, waging of war in the way of Allah, kindness to neighbours, orphans and dependents (whether they are mankind or animal kind), prayer, remembrance of Allah, recitation of the Qur'an, and similar other good deeds are but ingredients of worship. In the same way the love of Allah and His Prophet, hope of Divine blessings and fear of Divine wrath, fear of Allah, sincerity, patience, faith in Divine Decree, submission and pleasure in the will of Allah, all such good things are included in worship" (Al-Abudiyyat:2).

In the same speech, he later on said:

"While these verses bring to light the reality that submission is the zenith of any creature, they also reveal that religion is included in worship with all its constituents. All the Prophets came to mankind to preach the Divine religion. This is a fact which is mentioned in the Qur'an at numerous places. Every Prophet exhorted his people in the words "worship Him". It shows that "religion" and "worship" are two interpretations of the same thing.

All these details do not leave any doubt about the fact that Worship is the name of following complete religion. It cannot be said of any part of religion, whether it is of the nature of prayer or otherwise, that it is not worship. The fact is that we can acquit ourselves of true worship if we comply with the full code of religious injunctions. It is a unit which cannot be split any further. It is just like the human body which is a complete unit and cannot be split into more parts.

Special Importance of Pillars of Islam

Although consisting of various parts the human body is a complete unit. The importance of all its parts is not equal. Similarly, worship consists of a large number of constituents. All of them do not have an equal degree of importance and value. Some of them hold a special position as do the major parts of human body i.e., heart, brain etc. The special constituents of Islam are, those which are known as pillars of Islam i.e., Prescribed Prayer, Fast, Pilgrimage and Zakat (poor-due). The reasons why they hold a special position are given below:

1. They have a direct concern with the real Creator. In fact they are directed towards none but Allah. In their performance man is on the one side and Allah is on the other. In performance of all other acts the situation is quite different. Although other acts are also for the sake of Allah and are meant to win His pleasure, but in their performance someone does intervene between m an and Allah, and without that intermediary the act does not mature. When man is engaged in the performance of the prescribed prayer he has a direct link with Allah but hen he is

acting as a judge and passing judgements he is in a different situation. While praying he is directly in communion with Allah and there is no one to interfere. But while he is acting as a judge what actually happens is that although his mind is occupied in obeying Islamic injunctions and winning the pleasure of Allah, it is at the same time busy dealing with the people also. And as far as his tongue, ears and eyes are concerned, they are engrossed in the affairs of the people.

2. The pillars of Islam have a form of their own. They bear a stamp of worship and at a glance one is convinced that they are acts of worship and nothing else. Other acts are not of this type because they do not bear any such impress and one's mind does not immediately perceive that they are acts of worship.

3. The pillars of Islam have a special quality of cultivating a passion for submission and obedience, a quality which other acts do not possess in an equal degree. Although other acts too have this quality that their performance purifies one's self, renews in him the passion for prayer and invigorates his communion with Allah but the case, the profusion and the directness with which the spiritual wealth is generated in the normal circumstances by these pillars of Islam does not result from other acts. It would be more true to say that without the pillars of Islam that strength is not created which is but essential for the observance of standard worship. This is why they have been made compulsory and their decorum and rules have been expressly defined so that this source of strength is available to every Muslim and he can avail himself of it in the performance of real and complete worship. Pillars of Islam are no doubt constituents of worship but they are such that the life of other constituents depends on them.

If the distinction of the Pillars of Islam is kept in view it will be observed that they have a special relationship with the term worship. This relationship gives them a special privilege so that the term

'worship' primarily applies to them. When this term is mentioned
one's mind immediately turns to them. So much so that if the
distinction of these pillars of Islam is to be manifested they may even
be designated as 'absolute worship', and when the word worship is
used it is meant to indicate them. This is what has been actually done
and it is by no means an improper and unscholarly way of interpretation. It is in line with the accepted principle of nomenclature. On
the basis of this very principle the name Islam is specified for the
ultimate Divine religion although all other Divine religions also are
in fact nothing but Islam. This principle also applies here. The
compliance of every religious injunction is worship, but because of
the distinctive qualities of the prescribed prayers, fast, pilgrimage and
zakat (poor-due), they too are acts of worship. The purpose of doing
so is to highlight their distinction and special importance in the whole
system of worship. It would be absurd to think that the acts of
worship are limited to the pillars of Islam only and the rest of
religion is outside the boundaries of worship.

Misunderstanding and the Reasons for it

The real and comprehensive meanings of worship founded on the
authority of sound reasoning, evidence of the Qur'an and the research
of the religious scholars have been in the foregoing paragraphs. This
is just one point of view. The other point of view is that worship is
the name of prayer only. The Prescribed Prayer, Fast etc., fall in the
category of prayer and the rest of the religion is outside the orbit of
worship. Religion has a number of branches and worship is one of
them. This misconception, which is not only embedded in the minds
of the ordinary people but of the elite also has had far-reaching
effects. It cannot be overlooked as a trivial affair. There is actually
an urgent need to look into it to discover how this idea emerged and
how the people who entertain it have committed such a blunder
when everything should have been crystal-clear. This question will
also reveal why a refutation is so necessary.

The reasons for this misconception are psychological rather than intellectual. They are as follows :

1. This limited idea of worship is in vogue in the entire domain of
    prevalent religions and Islam alone is an exception to it.
    Worship and prayer are synonymous in religions other than
    Islam. In many of them it is considered unseemly, so far as
    worship and devotion is concerned, to perform any such act
    outside the sacred precincts. A concept which is so widespread
    acquires a quality of domination and it is not easy to save even
    those minds from its influence which should otherwise regard it
    as false. This is particularly true of those minds which have
    fallen a prey to intellectual decadence. In such a situation their
    own thoughts do not have the vitality to resist the onslaught of
    alien ideas. Islamic history presents several such instances. As
    long as Islam prevailed in the intellectual world as a dominant
    force, the un-Islamic ideas kept losing ground in their native
    lands and could not influence the Islamic intellectual world.
    When this situation was gradually changed the Muslims lost the
    illustrious position and threw their doors wide open to alien
    ideas. So much so that now they have reached a stage where
    innumerable un-Islamic ideas have assumed an Islamic colour.
    The worst part of it is that even the purity of the meaning of the
    most important Islamic terms has not survived. The words are
    no doubt the same which were given by Allah and His Prophet
    s.a.w. but their original meanings have changed. In this situation
    it is quite probable that the term worship also passed through
    this process of intellectual decay and the limited meanings of the
    term worship which were popular among other people also
    became acceptable to the Muslims.

2. The Prescribed Prayer, Fasting and similar other religious acts
    of Islam were so dazzling that they made people oblivious of
    other things. It will be admitted that the distinctive qualities of
    these acts (Pillars of Islam), enumerated above, are so
    fascinating that they can very easily derail one from the right

course of thinking. If some constituents of worship are such that their aspects, both inward and outward, are decked with special qualities and show a special link between the worshipper and the worshipped, and have no parallel in creating a passion for submission and accentuating religious fervour, and if they have a perfect appearance of worship also, then it is quite possible that some people may take them alone for worship. If the comprehensive conception of Islamic worship is not well-established in the minds it is quite likely that one may take these few things as worship and exclude all other religious acts from the realm of worship. It is not only likely to happen, but perhaps practically this alone is liable to happen.

Apparently these are the reasons which have subscribed to this misconception, otherwise, there is no rational or formal argument which can be advanced in support of this view.

14

ISLAM AND OTHER RELIGIONS

Concept of the Homogeneity of Religions

One thing gaining great popularity and importance in the present day religious world is the idea of homogeneity of religions. The essence of this idea is that all religions are true, all of them lead to God and all of them are equally successful in helping one to attain welfare and salvation in the After-life. The argument advanced in support of this idea is that whatever be the mode of prayer as long as one believes in God, its value and importance should be equal. What is of real importance is the spirit and not the form. Therefore, the mode of worship one adopts is immaterial. All that really matters is the object of worship. What we have to take into account in worship is that in whose remembrance is the worshipper lost whose manifestations is he eager to witness and whose pleasure is he craving to win. If the Hindu, the Muslim, the Christian, the Parsi and the Buddhist worship God in their own way and their ultimate goal is none else but Allah, then however different their apparent modes of worship and rituals are, they would still be worshipping Him only. All of them would be seeking Allah in their worship and as such all of them would be on the right path.

This idea determines the status of all religions. So it does of Islam. It holds Islam as a true religion but it does not regard Islam alone as the true one. It regards other religions as being equally truthful and upright. Is this position acceptable to Islam? It is a question which must be answered. It is not an ordinary question which may be ignored because it concerns the position of Islam and its answer will have far-reaching effects. This situation makes it clear that the proper knowledge of Islam would not be attained unless we know Islam's own decision in regard to this concept. The need for this knowledge becomes all the more essential when we see that some persons contend that the purpose and history of Prophethood mentioned in the Qur'an do not go against this viewpoint. They maintain that to an extent the Qur'an endorses this concept. It admits that Allah raised Prophets in every nation and all the Prophets and their religions were sent by Him. It even says that in their essence each of these religions was Islam. In these circumstances one should not deny that whichever religion is adopted and whoever Prophet is followed, it will be worship of Allah and would be sufficient for salvation in the Hereafter. Hence it is not necessary that everybody should obey the Qur'an and Islam.

Pre-eminence of the Prophethood of Muhammad *s.a.w.*

It is but evident that the pre-eminence of the Prophethood of Muhammad *s.a.w.* is in fact a part of the issue of Prophethood. In respect of this conception Islam's own decision about its own position will apply to the Prophethood of Muhammad *s.a.w.* If the position of his Prophethood is exactly similar to the previous ones the Qur'an will bear it out. If it is otherwise, and it does not consider the position of Islam identical with religions preceding it, then its decision will also be naturally different. We must, therefore, first of all find out the position of Islam. Is it similar to the other religions or is it different from them? The study of the Qur'an and the Tradition reveals that it is not similar to other religions. The Prophethood of Muhammad *s.a.w.* is distinguished in many ways:

1.   The first distinction lies in the fact that it is universal. Muhammad *s.a.w.* was not sent to any particular country or community but to the whole world and the entire mankind. He Who sent all the Prophets (*a.s.*) as well as Muhammad s.a.w. declares:

> *And We have not sent thee (O Muhammad) save as a bringer of good tidings and a warner unto all mankind but most of*

mankind know not (34:28).

Say (O Muhammad): O Mankind! Lo! I am the messenger of Allah to you all (7:158).

This is something exclusive for Muhammad *s.a.w.* None of his predecessors enjoyed such distinction. None of them was sent for the whole world or all mankind. Each of them had a limited sphere. If at all the missionary activities of any of them expanded further, they embraced only the immediately neighbouring lands. But this expansion was by way of a supplementary activity, otherwise they were commissioned to address their own people only. The Prophet Muhammad *s.a.w.* has stated in very clear words:

"Every Prophet who preceded me was sent especially to his own people but I have been sent as a Prophet for all mankind" (*Bukhari and Muslim*).

2.   The second distinction of his Prophethood lies in the fact that it is eternal, in the same way as it is universal. With him *s.a.w.* the chain of revelation (*Wahy*) and Prophethood (*Risalah*) has come to an end. No other Prophet will now come for all eternity. Allah has revealed this fact in clear-cut words in the Qur'an:

But he is the Messenger of Allah and the last of the Prophets (33:40).

The Arabic word used here is "*Khatim*" which means seal. When the seal is fixed on an envelope or on a document nothing can be added to it. Any such thing becomes impossible. Thus when Allah designates the Prophet Muhammad *s.a.w.* as the "seal of all the Prophets" it is an express declaration that the Prophethood is now closed and this last of the Prophets is being sent with Divine message till the Day of Resurrection and no one will be sent as Prophet after him. This information has been imparted to us by the Prophet himself on various occasions in unequivocal words. For instance:

"With me, the edifice of the Prophethood has been completed

and with me the chain of Prophethood has come to an end"
(*Bukhari*).

"No doubt, no Prophet will come after me" (*Bukhari and
Muslim*).

As compared to this how different is the case of the other
Prophets! It is something so abundantly clear that it needs no mention
or elaboration. Among the predecessors of Muhammad *s.a.w.* there
was no one who was not succeeded by another Prophet. It means that
their Prophethood was as much limited in time as it was in territory.

3.   The third mark of distinction of the Prophethood of Muhammad
s.a.w. is that the religion and Divine law which he has brought is
perfect in every respect. None of the religions and Divine laws
brought by his predecessors had this distinction. There is no doubt
that every Divine religion was sent by Allah but this Divine
declaration was withheld till the coming of this religion.

*This day have I perfected your religion for you and completed
My favour unto you* (5:3).

Thus this distinction was reserved only for Islam. It does not,
however, mean that other religions should be deemed imperfect. Nor
should it be considered that they wore not capable of providing
guidance to the people to whom they were sent. Such an idea will be
altogether absurd. On the contrary, each of these Divine religions was
sufficient for the betterment and guidance of the society, age and
country to which it was sent. As each of them was meant for a
particular community, country and era, and not for all mankind and
all ages, none of them contained instructions regarding the temporal
affairs. Nor did the teachings of any of these religions have a
universal character. Nor any of them addressed itself to the problems
of the future. As the mission of each of them was restricted to a
particular society its code of teachings was also brief and limited.
When it was ordained by Allah that such a Prophet be sent into the
world who should be for all, mankind and for ever it was but natural

to decide that the religion of such a Prophet should be of a universal character and its teachings should cover all times, all countries and all kinds of human problems. The verse of the Holy Qur'an cited above makes a declaration to this effect. The intention of this declaration was that the Divine guidance which started from the times of Adam (*a.s.*), and which continued to acquire a colour of detail and depth with the intellectual and cultural development of humanity, attained perfection that day.

4.   The fourth distinction of the Prophethood of Muhammad *s.a.w.* is that every word of the Book which was given to him is safe and would remain so till Doomsday. Not to speak of a word, even a single dot has not been altered in it. It is a Divine promise that:

> *Lo! We, even We, reveal the reminder, and Lo! We, verily are its Guardians* (15:9).

The claim that the Qur'an is safe from every kind of alteration is not a mere freak of blind faith. It is a fact borne out by history. Memorising the Qur'an by heart or its recitation alone do not guarantee that this characteristic of the Qur'an will remain unimpaired till eternity, the cultural conditions also subscribe to this belief.

The Qur'an happens to be in a language which is a living one. Millions of people speak this language and many more know, understand and teach it throughout the world.

As compared to the Qur'an there is no other book in the world that has this characteristic and which exists exactly in the same language and words in which it originally came to its Prophet and whose language is even today a living one. The condition of most of the Divine books is such that not even a single part of them exists in its original shape today. Many of the books which survive have been altered beyond recognition. They have been subjected to constant changes and alterations. Not to speak of the Books of ancient or prehistoric times, even those relating to the period of recorded history have not been preserved in their original form. Their followers have changed their language and a major portion of their teachings have beer forgotten by them. The Qur'an says:

> *They change words from their context and forget a part of that whereof they were admonished* (5:13).

NATURAL CONSEQUENCES OF THE PRE-EMINENT POSITION OF THE PROPHETHOOD OF MUHAMMAD
(*Sallallahu 'alaihi wasallam*)

If we keep in view the pre-eminent position of the Prophethood of Muhammad *s.a.w.* and compare it with others, we will be in a position to understand the natural consequences of this position of Islam. Does it deserve to be treated at par with the others despite its distinctions stated above and does it have the same prerogatives which other religions have? Answer to this question provided by sense and judgement and the Qur'an and the Tradition is in the negative. In their opinion the natural consequences of these facts will be entirely different. These would be as follows:

1.   Islam Alone Deserves to be followed

The first and foremost outcome of the pre-eminent position of Islam is that all the other religions have been abrogated and now Islam is the only religion approved by Allah. Therefore it is incumbent on people belonging to every nation, country and age that they should follow Islam because when this religion is for all mankind and its Messenger has been regarded as the Prophet of humanity, the religion or reign of any other Prophet, ceases to exist. A Prophet is sent unto a people so that they accept him as a Divine Messenger and follow him unconditionally. It is an admitted principle that:

> *We sent no Messenger save that he should be obeyed by Allah's*

leave (4:64).

The Prophet of Islam *s.a.w.* will not be an exception to this principle. There is no reason why it should not apply in the same way as it was all along applied in the case of other Prophets (*a.s.*). As such his appointment as a Prophet for all mankind, and his position of being the last of the Prophets openly warrants that not only all men but men of all ages have faith in his Prophethood, and follow it. If someone does not accept his Prophethood and refuses to obey the religion brought by him it would not merely be a revolt against him but against the Creator of the universe who sent him as a Guide and the last of His Prophets to the whole world.

When there is no scripture, except the Qur'an, which has remained safe from alteration, and the original language of which has not become dead, how is it possible to faithfully follow any other? This situation is an indirect corroboration of other Divine Books and Religions to the effect that their age has passed and they have been abrogated.

All that has been stated in the above paragraphs was a verdict of good sense and sound judgement. Let us now see what is Islam's own verdict on this issue:

Lo! religion with Allah is Islam (3:19).

And whoso seeketh as religion other than Islam, it will not be accepted from him (3:85).

The wording of these two verses is absolutely clear and reveals the whole situation. The verdict of the first verse that "the Religion with Allah is Islam" is quite clear but that of the second verse, which says that the religion other than Islam will not be accepted and that if any other religion is followed it will not be regarded as worship of Allah, makes it still more clear.

It would be wrong to assume that in these two verses the word Islam is used in its ordinary sense and not in its technical sense and as such it denotes every Divine Religion and its obedience. There is no possibility of such meanings because the word used here is "al-Islam" and not "Islam". The principle of Arabic language warrants that when the Qur'an uses the word "Al-Islam" it does not denote its literal or ordinary meaning but the technical one.

But even if this contention is not accepted (although it, would be wrong to do so) it will not effect the arguments given above. They will still hold good because in that case the meanings of these verses will be that the true and acceptable religion with Allah is that He should be perfectly obeyed and one must surrender himself completely unto Him. What would be the outcome and practical result of such an interpretation? Would it be different from the one contended above? No, certainly not. The reason being that after the coming of the Prophet Muhammad s.a.w. as universal Prophet, the correct form of perfect submission and complete surrender to Allah is to have faith in him and obey him s.a.w. Allah has notified in the Qur'an that the Prophethood of Muhammad s.a.w. is universal and eternal. If someone does not have faith in his Prophethood or in spite of accepting him as true Prophet, does not follow him, it would not be complete obedience to Allah. It will be simply the obedience of one's own self and would be regarded as an open defiance of Allah.

The proof of the fact that obedience of Islam alone is essential is also found in the actions of the Prophet Muhammad s.a.w. and it is a proof to which submission is inevitable unless one was prone to sheer injustice and self-love. If the concept, that all the religions are true and the obedience of every Prophet is equally important, is upheld by the Qur'an, its logical consequence should have been that the Prophet Muhammad s.a.w. would not have invited the Jews and the Christians to embrace Islam because they wore already the followers of Divine Books. If he had extended invitation to them he would not have insisted upon his invitation. On the contrary, he would have asked them to follow the Torah and the Bible faithfully. But it is an established fact that he did not do so. He invited them to embrace Islam exactly in the same way as he did the other Arabs who disbelieved in Allah. He made it as much compulsory for the former as he did for the latter:

O ye unto whom the Scripture bath been given! Believe in what We have revealed confirming that which ye, possess before We destroy countenances so as to confound them or curse (4:47).

He not only invited them to embrace Islam but regarded the disbelievers as people who had committed infidelity and we fit for Hell. So much so that on certain occasions their refusal to embrace Islam has not been described as disbelief but as disbelief of the worst kind. They have been held not as disbelievers but confirmed disbelievers:

Lo! Those who disbelieve in Allah and His messengers and seek to make distinction between Allah and His Messengers and say: We believe in some and disbelieve in others, and seek to choose a way in between; such are disbelievers in truth; and for disbelievers We prepare a shameful doom (4:150-151).

The reason for calling the people of the Scriptures "disbelievers in truth" in this verse was that while they believed in the other Prophets they were not prepared to accept Muhammad (peace & blessings be upon him) as the Prophet of Allah. He was the Prophet of Allah in the same way as were the other Prophets. This attitude has been described as an attempt on their part to "seek to choose a way in between" because on the one hand they were, by their belief in the other Prophets of Allah, fulfilling the requirement of belief in Allah, but on the other they were also defying His Godhood and Lordship by their refusal to accept the Prophethood of Muhammad (peace & blessings be upon him). This attitude has also been regarded as "disbelief in Allah and His Prophets" because. such discrimination in the acceptance of Prophets is in fact tantamount to believing neither in Allah nor in His Prophet. It is like bowing down to one's own whims.

On another occasion the Qur'an has mentioned this conduct of the people of Scriptures and commented upon it in the following words:

> *And when it is said unto them: Believe in that which Allah hath revealed, they say: We believe in that which was revealed unto us. And they disbelieve in that which cometh after it* (2:91).

What they said in response to the invitation to Islam needs careful attention. That is exactly the philosophy on which the idea of homogeneity of religions is now based. Its believers contend "when we are also endowed with a Divine religion is it not sufficient for us that we have faith in it and obey it? Why is it, after all, necessary for us to accept and follow something else when what we believe is as truthful as the one we are being asked to believe in"? But it will be observed that this philosophy of theirs is not only held as false by Allah but is expressly regarded as a philosophy of disbelief by Him. In spite of the fact that they hold their own religion as well as those of others as truthful He regards them 'disbelievers of the real truth.'

In short the refusal of the people of the Scripture to embrace Islam has been held by the Qur'an to be of exactly the same nature as that of the other disbelievers. It also holds that the consequences for both categories of disbelievers are similar. It has not made any such provision that even if they stick to their own religion their faith would be acceptable to Allah.

This matter does not end here. The Prophet (peace & blessings be upon him) has stated:

> "Had Moses been alive, even he would have no alternative except to follow me." (*Mishkat*).

This question of the Prophet *s.a.w.* makes this issue crystal clear and does not need further elaboration. A Prophet who has such an illustrious position that had other Prophets been alive during his age they too would have been his followers and would not have the option of following their own religion, how is it possible that ordinary men can be exempted from the responsibility of his obedience? In the presence of religion brought by him how could anyone be allowed to follow any other?

2. Islam a Pre-Condition for Salvation

The second essential consequence of these distinctive features of the Prophethood of Muhammad *s.a.w.* is that salvation in the Afterlife depends upon Islam. Since it is obligatory for everyone to follow Islam and other religions are no longer approved by acceptable to Allah, and it means that Islam is a must for salvation. Now let us see how Allah would treat those who follow a religion which He has Himself cancelled and declared unacceptable. After saying: *And whoso seeketh a religion other than Islam it will not be accepted from him* (3:85), Allah immediately declares: *And he will be a loser in the Hereafter* (3:85).

The Prophet *s.a.w.* elaborated this decision of Allah when he said:

"By One in Whose hand is the life of Muhammad, to whomever reaches the message of my to Prophethood be he a Jew or a Christian, if he does not affirm faith in what I have been sent with he would be one of the denizens of hell fire."

Although the names of the Jews and Christians alone have been mentioned in this tradition, but their names are cited for example's sake only. Its actual meaning is as plain as daylight, a universal truth. No community, no nation and no religious sect is exempted from this obligation. This is not a mere inference but a hard fact based on the words of this tradition "Any one of this community".

Obviously the words "this community" denote the people invited to Islam. It refers to them among whom Muhammad *s.a.w.* has been sent as Prophet. It is a well known fact that the people referred to here are none other than all mankind. That is why this tradition does not leave any doubt about the fact that it is obligatory for everyone to have faith in him. It is obligatory for everyone who lived in his age or was born afterwards. This decision of Allah is as binding on others as it is on the Jews and the Christians. In a way the case of other communities and nations is much more important because among all the nations of the world only the Jews and the Christians are two such communities who have been pointedly described as "the People of the Scripture" by the Qur'an. They alone are described as followers of the Prophets of Allah and believers of Divine religions. If the salvation of even these two communities depends upon the obedience of Muhammad *s.a.w.* then it stands to reason that this obedience must be all the more important for those who do not come in the category of people whom the Qur'an designates as "People of the Scriptures" or "followers of the Divine religions".

In short so far Islam's own decision is concerned it says in very clear terms that obedience to it is obligatory and a pre requisite for the salvation of all mankind. Only such a person who has not received this message can be exempted from it. The Prophet *s.a.w.* has provided this exception by using the words: "Whosoever has not listened to me".

This provision has been made because in such circumstances one is helpless. As long as a person is helpless and he does not receive this message he remains absolved from the responsibility of its obedience. To hold anyone responsible in such situation would have sheer injustice. But those who do not have faith in Islam even after knowing it are made justifiably answerable for it. To let them go unpunished would be unfair because their refusal to submit to Islam is not an ordinary matter. It is a refusal of the greatest imaginable thing, a refusal of the greatest truth. It is a denial of the sovereignty of Allah. It would be a travesty of truth if an action against this offence is regarded as unjust and unreasonable. Is it possible to think of a ruler who gives complete liberty to his subjects to flout his orders, to disobey his vicegerent and to defy the laws enforced by him and allows them to obey such of his viceroys who have been retired by him and permits them to abide by the religions which have been abrogated by him?

How is it possible that he would not punish those who disobey a Prophet whom He has declared as the universal and eternal Messenger? How is it possible that He would not take such people to task who defy a religion which He has prescribed for all mankind? It would really be a strange type of submission and obedience that while Allah appoint a person "A" as His Messenger to mankind, to instruct them in His worship, obedience and pleasure, another person is chosen by the people in his place for the same purpose. The case would however be different if a man is unaware that "A" is the authorised viceroy of Allah. But how can the conduct of a man who knows His real nominee be justified but sill insists on following his own sweet will?

15

RESPONSIBILITIES OF THE MUSLIMS AS A NATION

Special Requirements of the Pre-eminent Position of Islam

So much for the salient features of Islam. Now we come to the question regarding the pre-eminent position of Islam and the claim made on its behalf i.e., it alone is a perfect religion, it is for all mankind, it is the ultimate religion and its obedience is indispensable for salvation in the Afterlife. As Islam has a pre-eminent position it stands to reason that it must have some special requirements too. One of its requirements is that its message is conveyed and perpetually publicised in every nook and corner of the world. It is continuously preached among every nation and its message carried to every individual. This has to be a perpetual and ceaseless exercise. If it goes by default the world will not know of the message until and unless all mankind is acquainted with its mission it cannot come to Islam's fold. Faith in Islam is obligatory for all mankind and disbelief in this faith would prove to be disastrous. In these circumstances would it not be unfair to deny them the knowledge of the Divine law and thereafter to take them to task for their ignorance? If obedience of Islam is obligatory for all mankind, acquaintance with Islam is also imperative. Failure to do so would be on the one hand sheer injustice to Islam, as it would by that default be rendered useless, and on the other hand it would be unfair to mankind as they would be deprived of a blessing on which their fate ultimately depends. As long as the Messenger of Islam *s.a.w.* was alive he perfectly acquitted himself of this obligation of his towards mankind. But this obligation calls for action even when he is no more among us and would continue to do so till Doomsday. As no Prophet shall ever come in future this duty cannot be shifted to anyone else.

The pre-eminent position of Islam makes its preaching an imperative obligation. It must be fulfilled. How should it be done is a question of paramount importance. It not only warrants a suitable practical solution, it also has to be such as is prescribed by Islam. As Islam is a Divine religion, and has been sent for all mankind and for all times, it must have an answer to this problem.

Special Responsibilities of the Muslims

When we consult the Qur'an for the solution of this problem we find it there at the very first glance, it is there with its full details. Its answer is as magnificent as the question. In the words of the Qur'an the answer is as follows:

> *Thus We have appointed you a middle nation, that ye may be witnesses against mankind and that the Messenger may be a witness against you* (2:143).

This Divine order determines the practical form of this solution. It is as follows:

1. The responsibility of conveying the message of Islam to mankind, which was discharged by the Prophet *s.a.w.* during his lifetime has now been entrusted to his followers. They are responsible for carrying out this mission as long as they are present in this world.

2. The message of Islam is not to be conveyed to others in the ordinary way of preaching. It is to be done in a manner wherein it attains the form of witness.

3. "To bear witness unto Islam" has specific meanings which are determined by the action of the Prophet *s.a.w.* It signifies that the Muslims will convey it to others as earnestly as the Prophet *s.a.w.* conveyed it to his companions (*r.a.*).

It leads us to the conclusion that while the religious communities of the past had only one responsibility i.e., of following their own religion faithfully, the responsibility of the Muslim community has been further increased. This additional responsibility is that the Muslims present Islam to the world in the best possible manner. The Prophet s.a.w. has set for his followers a practical example of it in his actions.

The fact is that although the Prophet Muhammad s.a.w. was designated and destined as a universal and eternal Divine Messenger, the practical scheme for the continuation of this mission was also devised by Allah. It was so arranged that the Prophet s.a.w. would train a group of his descendants for this purpose. They were to be so perfected in this faith and its conduct that they would bear witness of the truth in the same way as he s.a.w. himself did. This group would in turn train another as its successor to continue this mission in the next generation. And this process would continue till the Day of Doom. That is why when the Arab tribes started embracing Islam in very large numbers and a group of the trained companions of the Prophet was also formed, the mission of the Prophet s.a.w. was completed and he was summoned by Allah. After his death the mission of preaching Islam to the world outside Arabia was performed by that group of the Muslims who were declared as "witnesses unto people":

Thus We have appointed you a middle cation that. ye may be witnesses against mankind (2:143).

It transpires that though the Prophet s.a.w. actually appeared among the Arabs, he emerged before the rest of the world through that group of Muslims who were trained by him s.a.w. In pursuance of this tradition a group of Muslims is trained in each nation for this purpose. This is why, after his death, it has fallen to the share of the Muslim community to bear witness of the truth unto the world. This has to be done in the same spirit as it would have been done by the Prophet himself s.a.w. were he alive. In short the Muslim community collectively is the successor of the Prophet s.a.w. and as a community is entrusted with exactly the same mission which was assigned to the Prophet *s.a.w*. This responsibility of the Muslims is not an ordinary one. It is so great and onerous that it alone becomes the sole purpose of their existence. The Divine verdict clearly determines the position of this community. This fact is further elaborated in the verse of the Qur'an which says:

> *Ye are the best community that hath been raised up for mankind* (3:110).

These words make it abundantly clear that the Muslims are not like the nations which existed during different ages. It is a nation which has been made the guide and the guardian of all mankind and this is the first and the last objective of its existence. It would be agreed that a thing is valued as long as it fulfils the purpose of its existence and its worth is lost as soon as it loses its objective. This is why the value of this community depends upon the task of bearing witness unto mankind. It will be regarded "the good nation" only as long as it fulfils this mission. It will be deprived of these illustrious titles if it fails to do its duty. So much so that in the latter case it would not deserve to be called even by its original name i.e., the Muslims, because this is not a mere name but an adjective. It was so designated because its Islamic responsibilities were much more than the other nations. The following words of the Surah Hajj (the Pilgrimage) of the Qur'an need special attention in this connection:

> *He hath chosen you and hath not laid upon you in religion any hardship: The faith of your father, Ibrahim (is yours). He hath named you Muslims of old time and in this (Scripture) that the Messenger may be witness against mankind* (22:78).

The pre-eminent position and the special responsibilities of the Muslims are made plain in this verse. First of all let us take up the Arabic word "*Ijtabakum*". It is synonymous with the Arabic word "*Istafa*" which means to choose something better. This word has been commonly used for the Prophets. If such a word, which is ordinarily used for the choice made for the Prophets, is also used for a nation, it is indicative of the illustrious position of that nation. After, that we come to the words which mean: "He hath named you Muslims of old times", which reveal that this nation has been specially designated as Muslim. This title has not been given to them now but is age-old. It is another proof of the pre-eminent position of this nation. It means that as the joyful news of the coming of the last Prophet *s.a.w.* was given thousands of years before his actual appearance and the world was eagerly awaiting his arrival so was the case of his followers i.e., the Muslims. A long time had yet to pass before the appearance of this nation but its name, conduct and characteristics were announced. Obviously, it was not an ordinary declaration. It was the announcement or a joyful news. It furnishes yet another proof of its being an extraordinary nation because such early announcement of the coming of a person or nation is only made if it has an unusual importance.

Now we come to the third characteristic of this nation, which is mentioned in the words "and in this Scripture". These words reveal the objective and purpose for which this nation was given such an illustrious name and position. They were so designated for "choosing something better". It does not only provide a proof of the exalted position but also offers evidence of the onerous responsibilities reposed in this nation. It clearly means that this nation has been so designated because it has to perform deeds compatible with its name. Last of all in this verse occur the words: "That the Messenger may be a witness against mankind". These words provide an answer to the question: "What is precisely the purpose for which this nation has been selected and how is it to be accomplished?"

In short this verse not only tells the significance of the title and position of this nation but also provides its justification. It has been so placed and designated because of the duty entrusted to it. If it does its duty, it would be a "nation submissive" otherwise it will have only the semblance of being so.

If the witness of the true religion is the objective and purpose of this nation, as is abundantly clear from all these verses, it will also be answerable for it before Allah. When a Muslim shall be answerable to Allah for each of his individual responsibilities the Muslim community, as a whole, shall have to answer for its joint responsibility. Let it be known that it will be no ordinary accountability. In its nature it will be similar to the accountability of the Prophets in their capacity as Prophets. It would be so because, though not a Prophet in a technical sense, this nation has been assigned apostolic responsibilities. In regard to the accountability on the Day of Judgement the Qur'an says:

Then verily We shall question those unto whom (Our Messenger) hath been sent, and verily We shall question the Messengers (7:6).

It means that as ordinary men would be questioned about their response to the invitation of the Prophets similarly the Prophets would also be questioned: how did they convey the Divine religion to mankind and what response they had from it? When the Muslim nation has responsibilities similar to those of a Prophet, it would be quite logical if the same kind of questions are put to it. How hard shall that moment of accountability be if this duty is not performed properly! This accountability will become critical if, God forbid, it turns out that they not only failed to do full justice while bearing testimony of the true religion before mankind but also kept it hidden from it. It would be criminal on their part to shirk their duties so blatantly and Allah has given a clear warning on this account:

And who is more unjust than he who hideth a testimony which he hath received from Allah (2:140).

Meaning of the Testimony of Islam

What is this testimony of Islam: It is a pertinent question which may be asked here and an answer to which is imperative for the proper understanding of Islam. We have already discussed in brief that Islam or the true religion is pre-determined. Similarly is the case of the meanings of the testimony of Islam and its practical form. This determination comes from the conduct of the Prophet *s.a.w.* This precise responsibilities of the answer to such a vital question may not be deemed sufficient and requires further elaboration.

Ordinarily testimony means a true statement of a person before others in respect of an event or a thing consisting of what he knows for certain about it. In the religious context it means that Islam, as it is, should be revealed to the people. Its technical meanings, though similar, are very comprehensive and sublime. It can be interpreted in the light of the life of the Prophet *s.a.w.* in the following words:

> "Testimony of the truth has two aspects, one is verbal and the other is practical".

1.   *Verbal Evidence*

Verbal evidence means that everything in respect of Islam, right from its fundamental beliefs to its detailed injunctions, is conveyed to the non-Muslims in the most suitable manner. It should be so presented before them as to become an open book for them and they should not feel any difficulty whatsoever in understanding the faults of their own beliefs and grasping the glorious truth of Islam. A few things essential for the correct performance of' this task are the following:

Firstly, such arguments are advanced in regard to its fundamental beliefs which make their truth plain to them. The comprehensive and forceful arguments given by the Qur'an about the Unity of Allah, Prophethood of Muhammad *s.a.w.* and the Afterlife are of fundamental importance in the preaching of Islam. Similarly the Islamic injunctions covering various fields of life should be explained to them in detail. It should also be made obvious to them how nicely Islam solves the problems of life and how its obedience guarantees the welfare of the temporal life also.

Secondly, what is un-Islamic should be seriously and logically criticised. It is naturally important for this purpose that the thoughts and ideas of the present-day world religions, cultures, philosophies and systems followed by the non-Muslims are fully understood. Their thorough knowledge is imperative for the comprehension of the logical basis of their belief. On the strength of this knowledge a forceful contradiction of the un-Islamic ideas would become easier. This should be done in such a manner that their failings are fully exposed and those consequences of their beliefs and practices are highlighted which are in no way wholesome for the humanity at large. Logical contradiction of the un-Islamic beliefs and ideas is an imperative need for the testimony of Islam and without doing this the task at hand cannot be properly accomplished. The invitation to Islam is akin to a new construction and when this is done it is essential that new foundations are laid down for it. To build without first laying down the foundations would be rank folly. The walls of a building are constructed when its foundations are laid. If we want Islam to be firmly rooted in the minds and hearts of the people we must prepare the soil for it. Obviously, this soil can only be prepared by uprooting those false beliefs and ideas which are embedded in their minds since ages. A thing can only be kept in a vessel if it is empty, not other-wise. On the same analogy Islam can only take its place in a heart if it is purged of all other religions. The Qur'an did not consider it sufficient for its invitation to give arguments in support of the Unity of Allah, Prophethood of Muhammad s.a.w. and the After-life but also considered it essential to forcefully contradict the philosophies which pronounced multiplicity of God, denial of true religions and deviation from the righteousness and disbelief in the Prophethood and the Afterlife. It took notice of all forms of disbelief and denial and kept in its view the avenues through which these ideas had entered the minds of the disbelievers. It also took note of the arguments advanced in support of their beliefs and then laid the falsehood of their notions threadbare. It exposed the futility of their ideas and completely demolished them. It was then and only then that the three hundred and sixty idols of Ka'bah were pulled down and that condition arose which is described by the Qur'an in the following words:

The right direction is henceforth distinct from error (3:256).

Thirdly, the act of proving the righteousness of Islam and falsehood of un-Islamic beliefs should be done in a very amiable and up to date manner. It should be in the language in vogue and in the style which appeals to the minds of the people. The mode adopted for the purpose should be such as is considered acceptable for discussion and debate in this scientific age. This is important because the act of proving the righteousness of Islam, and falsehood of what is contrary to it, is not a mere academic contest. It is for the preaching and spread of the true religion. It would be agreed that such an exposition is useless which does not make things intelligible to its listener and such preaching is futile which does not leave an impress of its message on the hearts and minds of the audience. In order to achieve success in this endeavour one should always keep in view the mind and mood of the man he is addressing. The mode of discussion should be such as his audience relish. The Qur'an adopted for its invitation such language, style and more to which the Arabs were accustomed. On the one hand what it said was in "plain Arabic".

In eloquent Arabic language (26:195).

Not only the style employed by the Qur'an was magnificent, even its diction was consonant with the standards of the times and its expression lucid. It was done to eliminate every chance of confusion arising out of a literary style or form of expression. The Qur'an adopted a style which was precise and succinct and was imbued with captivating oratory because the Arabs were immensely fond of such a style. On the other hand it made use of the universal principles, natural laws and everyday phenomenon as it was an effective medium as well as a congenial mode of argument for the Arabs. For inviting people to Islam, Allah ordained the Prophet *s.a.w.*:

Call unto the way of thy Lord with wisdom and fair exhortation and reason with them in the better way (6:125).

All the three requirements were in fact the practical aspects of this basic injunction.

Fourthly, the invitation to Islam should not be motivated by any impulse of national pride, hostility and display of oratory. Whatever is said should emanate from devotion, sincerity and love of Allah. It should be stimulated by a sense of duty and welfare of mankind. It should come from a heart which grieves over the faults of people. The audience, should have a feeling that the preacher is not taking away anything from them but is giving something to them something which is truly great. The anxiety and passion for bringing people to the fold of Islam with which the Prophet *s.a.w.* was imbued, is mentioned in the following words of the Qur'an:

> *Yet it may be, if they believe not in this statement, that thou (Muhammad) wilt torment thy soul with grief over their footsteps* (18:6).

2.   *Practical Evidence*

Practical evidence is that what can be found in the life of one who preaches Islam. Every Muslim in his individual capacity and the Muslim nation as a whole should present a true example of Islam. They should have implicit faith in the Unity of Allah, the After-life and the Prophethood of Muhammad *s.a.w.* and this faith must be reflected in each of their actions. Their conduct should be in accordance with the Islamic injunctions and their affairs should be governed by the laws of the Qur'an and the Tradition.

Their social, economic and political activity, in short their entire life and its every sphere is governed by the rules laid down by Allah and the Prophet *s.a.w.* Such obedience will present a true picture of Islam. It would also demonstrate what kind of citizen, society and social order it can bring about.

The position of practical evidence has far greater significance and importance than the moral evidence. Primarily for the reason that it does not behove an individual or a community to preach a religion to others which it does not believe. Not only it would be unbecoming, it will have no effect also. Secondly, a great majority of the people, say as many as ninety per cent of them, understand the language or practical evidence only. Mere rational appeal is beyond their intelligence.

In this connection it does not seem necessary to elaborate here the conduct of the Holy Prophet *s.a.w.* It is a plain fact that when he invited the people to Islam, he had already become an embodiment of the faith. When he conveyed a Divine injunction to someone he himself first submitted to it.

This is the true standard and meaning of Islam. It is the scale whereby the endeavours of the Muslims will be measured. The closer they are to this standard the greater shall be their success, and the farther they are from it the more distant they will be from their ultimate goal.

16

IMPEDIMENTS AND THEIR IMPLICATIONS

This world is an abode of the good as well as of the evil. It contains both the forces and each of them enjoys the freedom of action. The result is that they are locked in a ceaseless battle. They continuously try to overpower one another. It is, therefore, natural that impediments are placed in the way of Islam. Not only the evidence of its followers is not accepted, it is not even tolerated. The history of every religion and the evidence of everyday experience bear it out. This situation loads us to the question as to how the Muslims should overcome these obstacles. Islam enjoins them to do their utmost for the removal of all kinds of obstacles. Such a strenuous effort as they make for the removal of obstacles in the way of Islam is called *"jihad fi Sabilillahi"* (warfare in the way of Allah). *Jihad* literally means to strive every nerve for the achievement of an object, to exhaust all one's energies for the attainment of an ideal. Therefore to strive in the way of Allah signifies that one should do everything he is capable of for the pleasure of Allah; for obedience of the Divine injunctions and for bearing witness of the Truth.

Obviously, the struggle one makes for the achievement of an object is closely related to the situation he is placed in. The nature of his circumstances determine the course of his action. It will be wrong to brand it as opportunism. It is something quite natural. Every struggle that one makes has a definite purpose. It is a means to an end and not an end by itself. This end is best served if the struggle made for it conforms to the prevailing circumstances, situation and environments. If this principle is not observed even the best effort may prove futile. Such a course will be simply unwise and what is unwise cannot be natural. What will be the most suitable course for 'warfare in the way of Allah' depends solely upon the nature of each situation. Islam has laid down the following three principal forms of *jihad* (warfare in the way of Allah) which can be adopted according to the exigencies of the circumstances:

(i)   Internal *jihad*.

(ii)   *Jihad* through knowledge and invitation.

(iii) *Jihad* through war.

1.   Internal *Jihad*

It enjoins war against such evils as may crop up within the Muslim society. Such evils should be nipped in the bud because they pose a big threat to the evidence of Islam. In fact they are a serious danger for Islam and the Holy Prophet *s.a.w.* has warned against them in the following words :

"Every Prophet who was raised by Allah before me did have such sincere followers and companions who faithfully adopted his faith and adhered to his teachings, But they were succeeded by such disloyal people whose actions were at variance with their preachings and who preached what was not enjoined by their religion. He who fights physically against such ones is a true believer. He who fights against them orally is also a true believer. He who feels repulsion against them in his heart is also a true believer but this is, of course, the last degree and there is not even a particle of faith after it" (*Muslim*).

Obviously, this saying of the Prophet *s.a.w.* is not in the nature of a news. It is an order, an injunction. Its purpose is to warn the Muslims that they too may face such conditions. It also prescribes the action they should take in such an event. This tradition makes two things quite clear:

Firstly, whatever vice or evil crops up in a Muslim society, an endeavour to eradicate it is *jihad*.

Secondly, the possible modes for the eradication of an evil and the degree of their excellence in faith.

The best way of combating an evil is to use physical force against it and completely crush it. If the courage to use physical force is in any way lacking, the verbal force is used for this purpose. The evil is openly condemned. People are advised,.admonished and warned of the displeasure of Allah and its consequences in the Afterlife. If all these tactics fail they should be censured and reprimanded.

If the courage to condemn it openly is also lacking then the most important thing is that one condemns the evil wholeheartedly. He gets so averse to the evil that even its thought grieves him. The evil becomes an eye sore for him. He craves that the evil should be wiped out. He prays that the man who is suffering from the evil is reclaimed. His conscience is restored and his faith awakened so that he develops a repulsion for the evil and emancipates himself from its curse.

These are the three practical methods of purging the Muslim society of all the evils and these are the only ones in fact possible. Each of these modes is *jihad*. Each of them is a part of the struggle for establishing the Truth and bearing witness to Islam. To strive for the Truth is nothing but *"jihad fi Sabilillah"* (warfare in the way of Allah).

The efforts for the eradication of evil which have been termed as *"jihad fi Sabilillah"* in the above mentioned tradition have also been called as *"Taghayyar-i-Munkar"* (Transformation of evils) in some of the traditions. For instance:

"Whoever of you sees an evil must change it with his hand. If he is not in a position to do so let him do it verbally. If he does not have the courage to do this much even, he should do it in his heart and this would be the lowest degree of faith" (*Muslim* quoted by *Mishkat*).

Such efforts have also been called 'forbidding of evil'. For example;

(1) *Enjoin good and forbid evil* (31:17).

(2) "Persuade each other for good acts and dissuade each other from evil deeds" (*Tirmidhi*).

All these instances lead us to the conclusion that "to strive against the bad elements of the Muslim Society" and "to reform their wrongs and evil ways" and "to dissuade them from evils" are in fact nothing but the different expressions of the same thing. We may choose whichever of these expressions we like, it will make no difference to the object we have in view.

One thing more which clearly emerges from these traditions is that *jihad* is the collective duty of the Muslim society. Neither the individuals nor the state are exempted from it. Each of them has a share in this great responsibility according to his own position. This point is further elaborated by the Qur'an. In respect of individuals it says:

And the believers, men and women, are protecting friends one of another, they enjoin the right and forbid the wrong (9:71).

It clearly means that "to enjoin the right and forbid the wrong" is an everlasting quality of the Muslims. It is a redeeming feature of Islam. Wherever a Muslim is present he will be found doing it unfailingly. He who is a Muslim must do so. In respect of Islamic State the Qur'an says:

(4) *Those who if We give them power in the land, establish worship and pay the poor-due and enjoin the good and forbid the evil* (22:41).

It means that as a Muslim in his ordinary and individual position cannot see an evil flourishing, similarly he will do the same when he comes into power. Eradication of evils will be the basic aim and prime object of his rule.

2. *Jihad* through Intelligence and Invitation

This form of *jihad* enjoins that the doubts expressed about Islam by the non-Muslims, the objections raised by the unbelievers and the arguments advanced by the infidels are so completely answered that no doubt, objection or argument leaves any ambiguity about any aspect of Islam. The Meccan period of the Holy Prophet's life was entirely one of *jihad*. Allah ordained the Holy Prophet *s.a.w.*

So obey not the disbelievers, but strive against them herewith (the Qur'an) with a great endeavour (25:22).

Strive against them herewith (the Qur'an) means that you should go on presenting those Qur'anic arguments before the unbelievers which make the righteousness of Islam evident to them and expose the futility of the arguments which the infidels advance in support of their disbelief. It implies that by the mode of argument imparted to you by the Qur'an you should make the failings of their contentions clear. You should continue this campaign until they run short of even their fictitious arguments and are compelled to give in.

The Holy Prophet *s.a.w.* has also regarded it *jihad* of the tongue (oral *jihad*). He once said:

"Wage war against the infidels with your wealth, your lives and your speech" (Abu Dawud).

In a *jihad* of this type one is armed with the weapon of reason and intelligence against his enemy. This war continues until all the intellectual and philosophic ramparts of the enemy are razed to the ground. Every branch of knowledge is to be utilised for this purpose. Theology, physics, history, culture, economics, politics, science, philosophy, in short, every kind of knowledge is to be employed

without exception. The manner in which the Qur'an dealt with the
objections and contentions of the Arabs hardly needs any
introduction. A glance at the Divine verdict will make it plain:

*And they bring thee no similitude but We bring thee the Truth
(as against it), and better (than their similitude) as argument*
(25:33).

The Qur'an has laid down a basic principle for fighting this type
of war. It enjoins:

And reason with them in the better way (16:125).

The quality of a method can be determined by the success it
attains. The right course and the Qur'anic way of discussion for Islam
can only be such as would bring the listener close to the preacher,
convince him of the veracity of his contention and open his heart for
accepting the Truth. This can only happen when the words spoken
are full of rational appeal and have full regard for the level of
understanding of the audience. Equally important is the spirit of the
language he uses. It must be infused with true passion and sincerity.

Another requisite of this *jihad* is patience and perseverance.
Though apparently supplementary in character, it has great
importance and is indispensable for the success of this endeavour. It
is a well known fact that invitation to Islam often does not receive a
welcome response. The infidels unto whom Islam is presented are not
so broad-minded and honest that they will listen to the preaching
with serenity and hold discussion with propriety. What often happens
is that the audience is carried away by its own prejudice and emotion
and a wrong sense of prestige impairs its vision. They will answer
the serious arguments and plausible reasoning with harsh language
and shocking demeanour. Who can employ a method more sincere,
more devoted and more sweet and reasonable than those of the
companions of the Holy Prophet *s.a.w.*but even they had to put up
with a situation which was unbearable. They were fore-warned of
such situation by Allah in the following words:

And ye will hear much wrong from those who were given the Scripture before you, and from the idolaters. But if ye persevere and ward off (evil) then that is the steadfast heart of things (3:186),

It is evident that this verbal evidence of Islam can raise a storm of trouble for the man who is offering it and would ravage him again and again. Often it happens that a well-wishing is rapid with savageness, a happy greeting is answered with abuses and sound arguments are replied with stones. The matter does not end here. A preacher may even be condemned to silence. But the evidence of Islam warrants that such impositions are to be ignored outright and mankind is to be persistently invited to the worship of his Creator. It should be done without any fear of rebuff and rebuke. However odd the circumstances, one should not think of making a compromise with the situation. The Holy Prophet *s.a.w.* was exhorted by Allah that in such an event:

So proclaim that you are commanded, and withdraw from the idolaters (15:941).

The truth of the matter is that invitation to Islam only then attains the level of *jihad* when it is performed in the midst of the storm of opposition.

3.   Physical *Jihad* or *Jihad* by means of Arms

Jihad with physical force is enjoined against those who obstruct the way of Islam. This has to continue until the way is cleared. It is the final aspect of *jihad* and its other name is *'Qital'* (fighting). Practically this is the most difficult and crucial form of *jihad* but it has great importance for the perpetuation of the religion. Its paramount importance was highlighted when it was first ordained by Allah:

Warfare is ordained for you, though it is hateful unto you; but it may happen that ye hate a thing which is good for you

(2:216).

How can this be good for Islam and the Muslims is made clear
in other verses wherein its purpose is defined.

*And fight them until persecution is no more and religion is for
Allah* (2:193).

The order for fighting has been given to bring the state of
mischief to an end and to clear the way for a life that is governed by
Divine injunctions and steeped in the remembrance of Allah. *'Fitna'*
is a technical term of the Qur'an and signifies a situation wherein
people are denied the right to follow Islam and stopped from
worshipping their real Master. It is a crime that has no parallel. So
much so that even the crime of murdering an innocent pales into
insignificance before it. The reason being that if a person is murdered
he is deprived of the short course of worldly life, whereas if a person
is stopped from the worship of Allah and he is prevented from
becoming a true slave of his Lord his real life is brought to ruin and
he is deprived of the eternal blessings in the After-life. There is no
denying the fact that both these things are abominable but if it conies
to a choice even a fool would not prefer the latter over the former.
This is the reason why when the Qur'an says :

Persecution is worse than slaughter (21:101).

It says something about which there can be no two opinions.
When the priority of submission to Allah over every other
conceivable thing is established, there remains no ground to challenge
the justification of a sacrifice for removing the obstructions created
in the way of Islam. No matter whether it is the sacrifice of one's
own life or that of the others.

Another verse of the Holy Qur'an amplifies the importance of
physical *jihad* in a different way. The verse says:

*Had it not been for Allah's repelling some men by means of
others, cloisters and churches   and oratories and mosques,*

wherein the name of Allah is off mentioned, would assuredly have been pulled down (22:40).

This verse makes it further clear that if the sword is not used for the religion and the mischief is not uprooted, the religion will perish. The evil-doers will make religious activity impossible and destroy every sign of the worship of Allah. This is the reason why the use of force is inevitable for the perpetuation of religion.

Forms of *Jihad* through War

The obstructions which the believers have been ordained to remove by means of force are not always similar in nature. Naturally the measures to tackle them cannot be similar either. A survey of these obstructions is shown that in principle they are of two kinds:

1. Obstructions concerning those who have already embraced Islam. Those who have come in the fold of Islam are teased and tortured for their offence of accepting the religion. They are compelled to abandon their new faith and physical force is used against them for this purpose.

2. Obstructions concerning the non-Muslims. Muslims are not permitted to present Islam to the non-Muslims or such a system is imposed on them wherein the non-Muslims do not get an opportunity to see Islam closely.

As these obstructions are of two kinds the *jihad* to tackle them is also of two types.

As far as the first kind of obstructions is concerned it is not only very hard and unpleasant but extremely aggressive also.

The steps taken for fighting it would be in the nature of defence. It would be, therefore, appropriate to call it a defensive war. At first Allah ordained the Muslims for this defensive war because the obstructions, for the removal of which they were ordered to wage war, had already manifested themselves. The Divine order stated:

Sanction is given unto those who fight because they have been wronged and Allah is indeed able to give them victory; those who have been driven from their homes unjustly because they said: Our Lord is Allah. (22:39, 40)

This verse was revealed to the Holy Prophet *s.a.w.* during the Medinite period. It contains the justification of the Divine order as well. The Muslims were permitted to raise arms against the Quraish of Mecca because they were subjected to aggression by them. They were permitted to wage war as they were attacked. This contention was persistently repeated as long as the state of war with Quraish continued. All the battles which were fought during that period were of defensive nature.

Before we discuss the kind of *jihad* suitable for the second type of obstructions it seems appropriate that its nature is examined in detail. In the previous pages we have already mentioned the position of Islam and "the duties of the Muslims". It has been made clear that Islam is meant for the whole world; Islam alone is truth and it is the precondition for salvation in the Hereafter. Everything other than Islam is either untrue or is not approved by Allah. Muslims are liable to fulfil the requirements of this position of Islam. They are responsible for conveying it to the whole world. They have been entrusted the duty of bearing witness of its truth. They are enjoined to make every possible effort to turn people into obedient and true slaves of Allah and save them from making a mess of their After-life by remaining far from Him. These two obligations openly warrant that the Muslim society does not confine itself within its own orbit but goes forth to convey the religion to every part of the world. It does not let anything obstruct its way. In its mission to disseminate Islam to every part of the world it does not compel such people whose hearts it fails to open, as such a compulsion would be of no avail, but it does not permit them to guard the minds and hearts of others or create an atmosphere in which they cannot see Islam closely. Obviously, such an atmosphere will not be available to Islam until the reins of society are not snatched from the hands of the un-Islamic forces and held by its own because the system which is imposed on human society has also a firm grip over the minds of the people, or at least tries to do so, and hardly leaves any chance for them to advert to any other system of thought and action. Therefore as long as an un-Islamic system dominates a society, politically and ideologically, their minds will remain closed towards Islam. Such a situation is likely to impede the advancement of Islam. This is how Islam views it. Anyone who appreciates the position of Islam stated above would also be obliged to endorse this view. If the present situation happens to be such that every political system in vogue obstructs the way of Islam, it signifies that Islam does not accept the right of any un-Islamic system to rule any part of the world and wants this right to rest exclusively not in the hands of the Muslim rulers but with itself. Force is to be used wherever its supremacy is challenged. This is the reason why the Qur'an which enjoined a defensive war for a long time ultimately proclaimed:

He it is who hath sent His Messenger with the guidance and the religion of Truth, that He may cause it to prevail over all religions, however much the disbelievers are averse (9:33).

"Cause it to prevail over all religions" stands to mean both ideological as well as political domination. This is the reason why along with the foregoing verse it was ordained:

And wage war on all the idolaters as they waged war on you (9:36).

The Holy Prophet *s.a.w.* has declared this *jihad* a never-ending requirement and responsibility of the Muslim and exhorted them in this behalf:

"*Jihad* will continue from my time until such time that the last of my followers fights with *Dajjal*. This *jihad* will neither be suspended because of the cruelty of a cruel ruler nor will it be suspended through the justice of any judicious ruler".

The Holy Prophet *s.a.w.* and the four caliphs (*r.a.*) extended invitation of Islam to the rulers outside Arabia. When this invitation was not accepted by them they were perforce brought under the supremacy of Islam. Their subjugation to Islamic order was effected in pursuance of this obligation and aim. Since this *jihad* was not in the nature of a defensive war but a positive action it can be termed as a positive *jihad*. In respect of this type of *jihad* two things should be borne clearly in mind.

Firstly, it is not the intention of this *jihad* to compel people to accept Islam. Acceptance of Islam is something which relates to the heart and the heart of a man cannot be forced to accept any thing. As such Islam cannot be forced upon any one. It has been frequently repeated in the Qur'an that had Allah desired that none among the mankind remain unbeliever He would have created them all as Muslims or would have compulsorily made them Muslims after their creation.

Had Allah willed, He could have guided all mankind (13:31).

He would not have deferred it to His Prophet or his followers to make them Muslims perforce. Since such an imposition was not in keeping with the objective of mankind's creation, it was avoided. Allah has openly declared that in the matter of religion man has been created free. He is not to be forced for it:

There is no compulsion in religion (2:256).

In such a situation how could He regard it fair that in the case of Islam the compulsion, not exercised by Him, was permitted to His Prophets and His worthy slaves? This Divine injunction makes it abundantly clear that no person will ever be compelled to accept Islam. Everyone enjoys complete freedom in this respect. He may accept Islam if he likes or reject it if he so desires.

Secondly, *jihad* is by no means a campaign to elevate a community to the position of the ruling class and to reduce the other to slavery. It has not even the remote concern with what is now called imperialism or capitalism. Rather quite contrary to it, it is a campaign for establishing the supremacy of some such truths on which rests the system of this whole universe and on the acceptance of which lies the welfare of mankind, both in this world and in the Hereafter. Those who have heralded the pre-eminence of these truths have themselves accepted their priority. Is it possible that such a society which is the most accomplished slave of the Greatest Master would ever make slaves of others? The supremacy of the fundamental truths, which this society is so eager to get accepted from others is not meant for any selfish motives. In fact, it is meant for the benefit of those invited to accept them. The proponents of these truths do not take away any thing from them but try to give something to them, as by doing so they provide them with an opportunity to see that truth closely wherein lie the pleasures of both the worlds. No doubt such a submission will be unpleasant for their sense of prestige but this is a wrong notion of prestige and harmful to their own interest and as such fit to be ignored completely.

Conditions for Physical *Jihad*

Physical *jihad*, whether it is defensive or positive in nature, cannot be made at whim. It is permissible under certain specific conditions. It will not be valid unless the conditions laid down for it are present. Such a war which is waged regardless of the prescribed preconditions will have no value. It will not be a *jihad* at all. Nor would it be entitled to any reward. It will be instead a cause for the displeasure of Allah.

The Pre-conditions of the physical *jihad* are as follow:

1. Those who go for *jihad* should be free and independent Muslims and must have a collective social system of their own and must be led by a caliph or Amir (Chief). In the absence of such a system any act of war (*jihad*) is forbidden. An act of war, even of a defensive nature, can only be taken in a free atmosphere

under the leadership of an authorised leader. This is the reason why the Holy Prophet *s.a.w.* was not permitted to raise arms in self-defence during the period of his stay in Mecca, when he was not free to carry out his missionary activities, although the aggression of the Quraish had reached its climax. Permission for *jihad* was granted after his migration to Medina when he was living in a free atmosphere and where, under his leadership, an organised Islamic State had emerged. Similar was the case of other Prophets (*a.s.*) whose invitation to Divine religion had entered the phase of physical *jihad*. As long as this condition is not fulfilled, to undergo tribulations and upheavals for the sake of religion, constitute real *jihad*.

2.   Sufficient force to combat with the enemy is available because the Divine Injunction repeatedly emphasises:

No one should be charged beyond his capacity (2:235).

On the basis of this principle it has been ordained in the Qur'an:

So keep your duty to Allah as best as you can (4:16).

3.   *Jihad* should be exclusively for the sake of Allah and the sole-aim of those engaged in *jihad* should be no other than the service of the religion and the glorification of Allah. The singular aim of those who participate in *jihad* should be eradication of evil and advancement of goodness and justice. All this struggle should be done with one and the only objective of winning the pleasure of Allah. They should have absolutely no other motive in that noble war. When the Holy Prophet *s.a.w.* was asked that different people fight for different motives; one fights for the booty, another fights for fame and the third one fights for the honour of his country, nation or tribe or some similar cause, out of them whose fighting is for the sake of Allah? He *s.a.w.* replied:

He who fights for the glorification of Allah's   name,   his fighting alone is for the sake of Allah (*Muslim & Bukhari: Quoted by Riazus Salihin*)

On another occasion someone asked the Holy Prophet *s.a.w.* "Messenger of Allah: If a man wishes to fight for Allah but at the same time has also some worldly gain in view, how will he be viewed by you?"

He *s.a.w.* replied:

"He will not get any reward" (Abu Dawud, Vol. 1).

Similarly he *s.a.w.* also declared the principle:

"He is not one of us who fights under some prejudice and he is not one of us who dies for some prejudice" (Abu Dawud).

The need for the first two preconditions is quite evident. The third precondition calls for some elaboration which is as follows:

Islam has enjoined *jihad* for the eradication of evil and mischief and for establishing goodness and worship of Allah. Is it possible that men who foster evil sentiments, and are thereby led to fighting, can establish virtue and worship of Allah through their fighting? Obviously not. Whatever such men will do would end in the substitution of one evil by the other. Such an action would not benefit the cause of Islam. It would rather cause damage to Islam. They will play this evil game in the name of Islam and as a consequence, people would go farther from Islam.

Importance of *Jihad* in the Religion

On *jihad* rests the life of the religion. It is something natural for Islam. As such its importance in the religion cannot be ordinary. Whenever the Qur'an enumerates the basic qualities of devout believers it invariably includes the quality of *jihad* as one of them. For instance

(1) *Those who believed and left their homes and strove for the cause*

of Allah, and those who took them in hand and helped them these are the believers in truth (8:74).

(2) *O ye who believe! Shall I show you a commerce that will save you from a painful doom? (that is) Ye should believe in Allah and His Messenger, and should strive for the cause of Allah with your wealth and your lives* (61:10-11).

The Qur'an cannot even think that without *jihad* "True Religion and Faith" is possible and salvation from painful doom in the Hereafter can be gained without it.

Although these verses make a mention of physical *jihad* only, but in principle other types of *jihad* are also included in the injunctions enjoined therein. It means that the type of *jihad* compatible with each situation is a standard of faith. Let us find out its details from the Divine injunctions:

Internal *Jihad*

First of all let us take up the internal *jihad*. It has already been stated that the Qur'an has regarded it a line of demarcation between belief and disbelief. The Holy Prophet *s.a.w.* has declared it a mark of faith. It is, therefore a unanimous verdict of the Qur'an and the Tradition that a heart which does not throb with the passion to spread good and stop evil is full of the darkness of disbelief. It is the basic quality of a true believer that he cannot tolerate the sight of an evil. If he cannot do anything against evil, if he is unable even to open his lips against it, he condemns it vehemently in his heart. This is, of course, the last and the lowest degree of faith. If a Muslim does not have even this much hatred for evil he is not reckoned a Muslim by Allah and His Prophet *s.a.w.*.

This type of (*jihad.*) is so closely and naturally related to belief that it has been made a standard for the life of nations. A nation whose pious men are all the time concerned with their own piety, and close their eyes to the storm of evils surrounding them, loses its value. Such a nation is burnt like the dry grass of jungle. When a calamity visits that nation it destroys both, the wicked as well as the pious who had done nothing to check the evil. A few who survive, if any, are saved only for the reason that they did not forget their duty amidst that storm and did their best to dissuade people from the evil. The history of ancient nations is in fact the story of the enforcement of his Divine law. While warning the Muslims of this Divine law, the Qur'an also comments on this phenomenon:

If only there had been among the generations before you men possessing a remnant (of good sense) to warn (their people) from corruption in the earth, as did a few of those whom We saved from them (11:116).

The Holy Prophet *s.a.w.* warned the Muslims of this Divine law of punishment and salvation and exhorted:

"By One in whose hand is my life you must enjoin the good and forbid evil or Allah would definitely send chastisement when you would supplicate Him but He would not respond you".

The above mentioned tradition and many other sayings of the Holy Prophet *s.a.w.* elaborate this Divine injunction:

And guard yourselves against a chastisement which cannot fall exclusively on those of you who are wrongdoers, and know that Allah is severe in punishment (8:25).

The severest chastisement befell the children of Israel only when they became negligent of their responsibility of making internal (*jihad.*). They had reached a stage where the evils were growing like wild plants and no worthwhile effort was made for their eradication. The Holy Qur'an describes this situation in the following verse:

Those of the children of Israel who went astray were cursed by the tongue of David, and of Jesus, son of Mary. That was because they rebelled and used to transgress. They restrained not one another from the wickedness they did. Verily evil was that they used to do (5:78-79)

This type of (*jihad.*)   is also very important as a positive testimony of truth. In a way it is of the highest importance as the success of the witness before the outside world actually depends upon his participation in the act of witness. If this is not done, and on the one hand efforts are made to prove the truthfulness of Islam and on the other the followers of Islam provide evidence of their practical love with the elements of disbelief, their testimony will become ineffective. In such a situation the world would deem it a mere display of the Muslims' pride and superiority. To a large extent the world will be justified for this impression. As such it is imperative that before the Muslims convey the message of Islam to others they themselves acquire the character of a naked sword against the evils thriving amidst them.

Jihad through Preaching and Reasoning

Let us now consider the importance of this (*jihad.*). If as a nation the life of the Muslim is meant to be the witness of Islam, as indeed it is, then because of its vital significance and vastness the value of this form of (*jihad.*) is extraordinary. Its need is more than evident. Unless Islam is presented to others in a befitting manner its evidence will not be complete. It is, therefore, necessary that Islam is presented to them with all its essentials. It should be expounded in a manner which satisfies all their inquisitions and doubts concerning Islam. As to its vastness it is by no means a secret. If Islam is one, its rivals are numerous. So far as formal introduction of Islam is concerned, a short discourse may be sufficient for it but witness of Islam is something quite different from it. Its significance is much more than the formal introduction of Islam. People before whom this witness is to be given are not the followers of the same faith and religion. They believe in different ideologies, needs, religious and political systems and the Muslims have to give witness of Islam before all of them. How onerous is the duty of bearing witness of Islam on so vast and diverse fronts. What a multitude of weapons is to be encountered in this war? How crucial are the campaigns to be won? Physical (*jihad.*) is done under specific conditions and in the presence of a variety of preconditions but this form of (*jihad.*) is not subject to any condition of time, environment and circumstances. It is a ceaseless struggle. A duty which calls for action everywhere, at all times, in all events and in every situation. It is an unending task. Until the situation is ripe for physical (*jihad.*), the struggle for upholding the truth depends entirely on this measure. The history of many of the Prophets reveals that the entire period of their prophethood was spent in this occupation and the stage to commence physical (*jihad.*) was never reached. This form of (*jihad.*) is in the real sense a (*jihad.*) with the outside world. Physical (*jihad.*) is a sequel to certain exigencies. The real aim of preaching the religion, and bearing witness of Islam, is to make people alive to the Infinite Greatness of Allah and infuse faith in them. This faith is achieved through good counsel and plausible reasoning and not by dint of sword. The sword is only raised to remove the obstacles created in the presentation of Islam.

This form of (*jihad.*) is so esteemed by Allah that He has regarded it as "His help" and those who are engaged in this world as "His helpers":

> *O ye who believe! Be Allah's helpers, even as Jesus son of Mary said unto the disciples: Who are my helpers for Allah? They said: We are Allah's helpers.* (61:14).

It is a well known fact that the invitation of Jesus could not enter the phase wherein the physical *(jihad.)* becomes obligatory. It was, therefore, restricted to preaching and reasoning. But even with this much of their struggle the companions of Jesus have been regarded as "helpers of Allah". It means that this, the most illustrious title, was given to them for the reason that they did full justice to conveying the religion of Allah to the people. Here the words "did full justice" deserve special attention as they stand to signify that the behaviour of "helpers of Allah" is given to the believers only when they devote all their energies and intelligence to convey the religion to others, when they go on repeating the message of religion in unfavourable circumstances and when they do not assume silence in the storm of dangers. It is not a speculation but a revelation of the Qur'an. The Surah III (Al-i 'Imran) of the Qur'an contains further details of this point. The Prophet Jesus (*a.s.*) uttered these words only when his audience, the children of Israel finally rejected him and their malicious activities against him were coming to a climax. The relevant verse of the Qur'an reads:

> *But when Jesus became conscious of their disbelief, he cried: Who will be my helpers in the cause of Allah? The disciples said: We will be Allah's helpers. We believe in Allah and bear thou witness that we have surrendered (unto Him)* (3:52).

It transpires from this verse that the decision of a believer's attaining the level of "helper of Allah" is made only when the invitation of religion goes beyond the level of preaching and reasoning and enters the phase of heavy opposition. Believers who do not sit tight-lipped and with forbearance convey the message of Allah to His People, are called "the helpers of Allah" because such endeavours constitute real (*jihad.*) and are meant for the "help of Allah's religion".

Physical *Jihad* by Means of Force

The pages of the Qur'an and the Traditions abound with the great merit of this act. Their study reveals that, except prayers, no other act is more popular with Allah than (*jihad.*). When those who in the teeth of opposition invite people to the Truth through preaching and reasoning, are called by Allah as "His helpers" what would be the status of those who go forth to sacrifice even the last of their wealth. Such men are not called by Him "His helpers" but "His loved ones":

> *Lo! Allah loveth those who battle for His cause in ranks as if they were a solid structure.* (61:4)

Some detail of this love is given in the sayings of the Holy

Prophet *s.a.w.*.

"The guarding of the frontiers for a day and night is more valuable than a month of fasting and prayer" (*Muslim*).

"The act of everyone who dies comes to an end with his death but the case of such a person is quite different who dies when he is about to encamp during the course of war, he is waging for the cause of Allah, because this act of his would continue to grow till the Last Day" (Tirmidhi).

"I swear by Him who holds the life of Muhammed in His Palm that a morning's or evening's journey for taking part in (*jihad.*) in the way of Allah is better than this world and all that it contains and staying in front of enemy is better than seventy years of prayer at home" (Tirmidhi).

"Those who go forth to (*jihad.*) their act is similar to the one who continues to keep fasts, say prayers and recite the Qur'an most steadfastly until the Mujahid (soldier) returns from (*jihad.*)" (*Muslim and Bukhari*).

Not only the war for the glorification of Allah's name makes a man eligible to His love, forgiveness and blessing, even those persons also get an illustrious position who help the warriors indirectly and lend assistance in the preparation for (*jihad.*). The Holy Prophet *s.a.w.* said:

"Anyone who provides material for war to any Mujahid (soldier) acts as though he himself participated in (*jihad.*) and anyone who looks after the family of a Mujahid (soldier) acts as if he himself took part in (*jihad.*)" (*Muslim and Bukhari*).

"Because of a single arrow Allah admit three persons in heaven, the man who makes the arrow with the intention of earning the blessings of Allah, the man who shoots it on the enemy and the man who supplies that arrow to him" (Abu Dawud).

If one who makes or provides the arrow for (*jihad.*) is given such a great reward, how would He reward him who goes forth from his home for His sake, fights on the battle-field and is wounded, sheds his blood and ultimately lays down his life for his Master? An idea of the good luck of such a person can be had from the following proclamation of Allah:

> *Think not of those who are slain in the way of Allah, as dead. Nay they are living. With their Lord they have provision. Jubilant are they because of that which Allah has bestowed upon them of His bounty. They rejoice because of the favour from Allah and that Allah wasteth not the wages of the believers* (3:169-171).

Let it be remembered that in the Holy Qur'an such heartening phrases have been used only for those who lay down their lives while fighting in the way of Allah. This special announcement of the Qur'an reveals that the love which He cherishes for this act is not ordinary but something exceptional. What the Prophet of Allah has stated in this respect offers some elaboration of this exceptional love. He *s.a.w.* said:

> "Anyone who will enter Heaven would not like to return to this world even if everything of this world is given in his ownership. But Shahid (martyr) will not be in this condition. When Shahid (martyr) will see the honour bestowed upon him by Allah he will desire that he returns to the world ten times and is slain in the way of Allah ten times" (*Muslim and Bukhari: Quoted by Riaz-us-Salihin*)

This is what will happen in the After-life. The Shahid gets a special distinction in this world as well. Everyone who does is given a bath and his clothes are replaced with a clean sheet of cloth (shroud) but there is an express injunction that the Shahids (martyrs) should neither be given a bath nor should they be wrapped in a shroud. They are to be buried in the very blood stained clothes in which they were slain. Hazrat 'Abbas (*r.a.*) stated:

"The Holy Prophet *s.a.w.* ordered about the Shahids (martyrs) that their weapons should be taken away and they should be buried as they are, with impediments and their bloodstained clothes and bleeding bodies" (Abu Dawud, Vol. 11)

The reason for this order is found in another tradition. It reveals that the blood of the Shahid is not the ordinary blood which is held as unclean by Islamic law. No other thing is more sacred than such a blood. It is a blood the cleanliness of which is unsurpassed. Allah holds it as beautiful as saffron and as fragrant as musk.

"Its colour is like saffron and it smells like musk" (Trimidhi, Abu Dawud: Quoted by Mishkat).

It is established on the authority of the Qur'an and the Tradition that the status of those who are slain in the way of Allah is distinctive and enviable in many respects. A careful consideration will disclose that this established fact points towards, and makes clear many other truths.

Firstly, physical (*jihad.*) is the best and the most venerated form of (*jihad.*). Secondly, it is the greatest act of piety, greatest act of prayer and the best form of worship of Allah. When the Holy Prophet *s.a.w.* was asked as to which was the best form of (*jihad.*), he *s.a.w.* replied:

"The best (*jihad.*) is that one should fight against the disbelievers with his wealth and life" (Abu Dawud).

Similarly when he *s.a.w.* was asked as to who was the best of men, he *s.a.w.* replied:

"The best of the believers is he who fights in the way of Allah with his wealth and his life" (*Bukhari and Muslim: Quoted by Riaz-us-Salihin*).

One who fights with his wealth and life is the best of the

believers. It would be just the saying if it is said that to fight in the way of Allah with one's life and wealth is the noblest of acts and the most meritorious deed. An act which ranks highest must logically be the most rewarding as well. The references from the Qur'an and the traditions quoted are indicative of this fact. The following traditions will further confirm it.

> " The fire of hell shall not touch the two types of eyes: Firstly, the eye that wept with the fear of Allah. Secondly, the eye which spent night as a sentinel in the way of Allah" (Trimidhi).

> "The dust that rises in (*jihad.*), made in the way of Allah, and the smoke of Hell cannot get together over anyone" (Trimidhi).

> "Who fought in the way of Allah, even if it was equal in duration to the pause that occurs between the two flows, in making a she-came!, must go to Heaven" (Tirmidhi).

In the Battle of Hunain a companion, Anas bin Abi Murthid Ghanavi (*r.a.*) kept a watch at a valley for the whole night. When he returned from his duty in the morning and came to the Holy Prophet *s.a.w.* he said unto him:

> "You have made Heaven inevitable for yourself. No matter even if you do not do any act of goodness after it" (Abu Dawud, Vol. I).

In respect of those who fought the Battle of Badr the Holy Prophet *s.a.w.* once said to the Caliph 'Umar (*r.a.*):

> "You know it not, perhaps Allah may have looked at the men of Badr and said: go and do whatever you like. I have blessed you" (*Bukhari, Vol. II*).

There is no reason for surprise if the physical (*jihad.*) has been ranked so high by Allah. It is a plain fact and merits no surprise.

If the worship of Allah is the sole aim of a believer's life, and the Muslim nation has been created exclusively for the purpose that it should bear full witness to the Truth before the whole world, then could there be a servitude better than this servitude and could there be a witness greater than this witness which is given at the cost of one's life? It is, therefore, beyond any shadow of doubt that it is the greatest servitude and the most valuable witness. In other words it may be said that (*jihad.*), is the perfect effort for the achievement of the objective set forth for a Muslim's life. When he sacrifices his life for this objective, his ultimate destination of submission to Allah and his duty of bearing witness to the Truth, is fully attained. The sacrifice of one's life is certainly the last thing which a man can offer for an objective. In fact only such a man deserves to be called the real flagbearer of that mission and the most faithful servant of that cause. This is the reason why although every Muslim who bears witness to the Truth, through his speech and act, is a *Shahid* (witness) of the religion but as far as the name or title is concerned it is reserved only for those who lay down their lives for the religion of Allah. Reason being that they are the people who sacrifice even their last thing and exhaust their final effort for the testimony of Islam. That is the reason why the title of Shahid behoves them and them only.

This discussion has also made it clear that the sacrifice of a life and wealth in the way of Allah is the zenith of a man's belief. When one embraces death on the battlefield pleasure of Allah he leaves no attainable height of faith unscaled. So much so that if till then his life has been a life of reform and piety, he attains a place, by virtue of this act of (*jihad.*), from where onward remains only one place which is specially for the special for the prophets. Utba ibn Abdus Salmi related:

"The Prophet of Allah said that the believers slain during the course of (*jihad.*) are of three kinds. Firstly, the believer who fights with his life in the way of Allah, encounters the enemy and fights with him till he is slain. In respect of a person who is so slain, the Holy Prophet *s.a.w.* told:

"Such is the true and confirmed Shahid (martyr). He will live in the canopy installed beneath the throne of Allah. The only distinction which the prophets will have over him will be the distinction of their prophethood" (Darimi).

One aspect of the religious importance of physical (*jihad.*) still remains unexplained and should also be made clear. What has been mentioned in the Qur'an regarding physical (*jihad.*) shows that from the religious and national point of view this (*jihad.*) does not have the same importance at all times. At one time it is only an act of distinction and valour and at another time it is a religious obligation and mark of faith. For further elaboration it may be stated that when there is no need to make a general call of (*jihad.*) to face the enemy and only a limited number of men is required to win the campaign, this military service will be an act of distinction. One who will render this service would be entitled to the reward and blessings stated above. Anyone who will not take part in this service would not be blamed for his non-participation. In such cases the Qur'an enjoins:

Unto each Allah hath promised good, but He bestowed on those who strive a great reward above the sedentary (4:95).

But when this is not the situation and the leader of the Muslim passes a general order of mobilisation then the war service does not remain a point of distinction only. Then it becomes an incumbent religious duty and a standard of faith. In the days of the Holy Prophet *s.a.w.* when some people, after the announcement of open war, showed slackness in going forth for (*jihad.*), they were expressly told:

O ye who believe! what aileth you that when it is said unto you: Go forth in the way of Allah ye are bowed down to the ground with heaviness. Take ye pleasure in the life of the world rather than in the Hereafter? If ye go not forth He will afflict you with a painful doom and will choose instead of you a folk other than you (9:38, 39).

Similarly those who made excuses and on one pretence or the other begged to be excused from participating in the action from the Holy Prophet *s.a.w.* were warned in these words:

> *Those who believe in Allah and the Last Day ask no leave of thee lest they should strive with their wealth and their lives. Allah is aware of those who keep their duty (unto Him). They alone ask leave of thee who believe not in Allah and the Last Day, and whose hearts feel doubt, so in their doubt they waver* (9:44-45).

These verses disclose that to shun (*jihad.*), when it is an incumbent duty, amounts to a violation of faith. It also transpires from these verses that to cherish the passion and will to fight in the way of Allah is an inseparable element of faith. It is altogether a different question as to when the occasion for this fight occurs and when the prerequisites of the (*jihad.*) are fulfilled. The action of a believer may await this occasion and the conditions thereof but his passion for (*jihad.*) cannot wait for it. He will be all the time anxious for it. The mind of a Muslim, if he is a true believer, will always be preoccupied with it. When he is summoned by an emergency, and the conditions required for it make it permissible, he would not sit quiet in his place. The following words of the Holy Prophet *s.a.w.* make the natural link between the faith and physical (*jihad.*) abundantly clear:

> A person who died in such a state that he neither fought for the religion, nor even thought of it, died in a degree of disbelief" (Muslim with reference to Mishkat).

The logic of this verdict of the Holy Prophet *s.a.w.* is evident. The community designated as Muslim has not been created to lead a life of its own choice like others. It has been created with a specific mission. So great and important is this mission that its performance demands from him everything he possesses. Only such a person can acquit himself of this duty who does not love anything, not even his own life, more than his mission. The true Muslim society is in fact such a group of individuals who possess this quality of sacrifice. In the absence of this quality it will be merely just another community or a society but not a Muslim society. It will not be able to perform the task for which it has been created. The decision of the Qur'an on this issue is before us. When some men, despite being Muslims, evaded the duty which was incumbent for them as Muslims, Allah censured them in the following:

> O ye who believe! Whoso of you becometh a renegade from his religion (know that in his stead) Allah will bring a people whom he loveth and who love Him, humble towards believers, stern towards disbelievers, striving in the way of Allah, and fearing not the blame of any blamer (5:54)

The meaning of this Divine injunction is obvious. Some qualities are essential for the type of men Allah needs for His religion. One of these qualities is *jihad.* in the way of Allah. Those who lack this quality cannot perform the duty of supporting and serving the religion and bearing witness to it. A Muslim who cannot perform this duty gets himself terminated from his position. It is for this reason that evasion of religious obligation has been described as "reversion from the religion". This warning has also been given in the verse of the Surat Tauba (Repentance) of the Qur'an mentioned above. It says :

> If you go not forth He will afflict you with a painful doom and choose instead of you a folk other than you (9:39).

Obviously, a man or a group is removed from his office only when he is no longer capable of it and he cannot perform the work assigned to him.

17

WORLDLY BLESSINGS OF ISLAM

Material Prosperity and the Apostolic Mission

From the general introduction of Islam given in the previous chapters one fact which comes repeatedly before us is that Islam is the name of living and dying for the pleasure of Allah alone. It emphasises that a Muslim is one who always keeps his eyes focused on the After-life and does not, at any cost, allow worldly gains to have priority over the welfare of the Afterlife. It is pertinent to ask here that when he is so placed that he has to devote himself completely to his religion, what sort of life is he going to lead? Would he be left with any worthwhile worldly object? Shall the Muslims be prosperous individually and command respect and power as a community? It is an ordinary question and need not arise in the case of Islam alone. It equally applies to other Divine religions because originally there was no difference in Islam and the other Divine religions. Like Islam every religion preached that the essence of religious life and the true spirit of worship of Allah was submission to Allah and preference of the Afterlife over the temporal life. It would, therefore, be better if before consulting the Qur'anic invitation we find out the answer to this question in other religions.

When we make a survey of other religions we do not find there the answer we expect. It is just the opposite. We see that each of those Prophets who invited their people to the Divine religion assured them that by following him they would not only earn the benefits of the After-life but of this world as well. The Prophet Nuh (*a.s.*) told his people:

> *Seek pardon of your Lord. Lo! He was ever forgiving. He will
> let loose the sky for you in plenteous rain. And will help you
> with wealth and sons, and will assign unto you Gardens and will
> assign unto you rivers* (71:10-12).

The words of the invitation of the Prophet Hud (*a.s.*) were as
follows :

> *And, O my people ask forgiveness of your Lord, then turn unto
> Him repentant; He will cause the sky to rain abundance on you
> and will add strength to your strength* (11:52).

The detail of this Divine promise and its full evidence can be
seen in the history of Israel which begins from the period preceding
a little before the birth of the Prophet Moses (*a.s.*). Since then until
the appearance of the Prophet their life was extremely wretched. It
changed for the better when they inclined towards their Creator and
showed steadfastness in the observance of His religion. The Qur'an
reveals:

> *And the fair word of the Lord was fulfilled for the children of
> Israel because of their endurance* (7:137)

Because of their inclination towards Allah and steadfastness on
the path of Truth their wretchedness was changed into prosperity. Not
only that, they were even assured of the principle that as their
gratefulness to Allah and observance of His injunctions increased
they will be blessed with more and more Divine favours.

> *And when Moses said unto his people: Remember Allah's favour
> unto you when He delivered you from Pharaoh's folk who were
> afflicting you with dreadful torment* (14:6).

> *And when your Lord proclaimed: If you give thanks, I will give
> you more* (14:7).

So long as they were grateful to Allah the world saw that the

Divine promise was fulfilled. It was fulfilled so magnificently that they attained the highest peak of national glory and no other nation of the world was able to come up to them in honour and prestige. Referring to this glorious period of their history Allah reminded them in the Qur'an:

O Children of Israel: Remember My favour wherewith I favoured you and how I preferred you to (all creatures) (2:47).

When they abandoned their attitude of gratefulness, submission and adherence to religion they were stripped of this role of honour. That is why they were in a miserable plight at the time when the Holy Prophet *s.a.w.* came to this world. This Qur'an commented on their condition in the following words:

If they had observed the Torah and the Gospel and that which was revealed unto them from their Lord they would surely have been nourished from above them and from beneath their feet (5:96).

What has been discussed above related to one particular nation or the other. Let us see the Divine proclamation in respect of all the nations:

And if the people of the township had believed and kept from evil, surely we should have opened for them blessings from the sky and from the earth (7:96).

This is a proclamation for those who digressed from the path of faith and worship of Allah and were not therefore eligible to the reward promised by Allah. The verdict in respect of those who adhered to the path of righteousness is given in the following words of the Qur'an:

So Allah gave them the reward of the world and the good reward of the Hereafter (3:148).

The examples of the Prophetic missions are before us. They

signify an unalterable principle and decision of Allah that for submission and obedience unto Him Allah will not only grant prosperity in the Hereafter but endow upon them affluence, honour and power in this world as well. These illustrations also reveal that whenever a nation adopted the way of obedience and submission, the Divine promise and principle were unfailingly fulfilled. Not only the welfare of their After-life was assured, they thrived in this world also.

Islam Guarantees the Welfare of the Temporal World

There is no reason why the Divine verdict should have changed in the rise of Islam and its followers. It has not changed. In respect of the material prosperity, a promise exactly similar to the one made persistently with all the other nations was made with the Muslims as well. This promise was made during the depressing situation of the Holy Prophet's life at Mecca and in the dangerous circumstances of his stay at Medina. It was given to those who had not yet embraced Islam as well as to those who had embraced it. When the citizens of Mecca were invited to Islam they were told in very clear terms by Allah:

> And (bidding you) ask pardon of your Lord and turn to him repentant. He will cause you to enjoy a fair estate until a time appointed (11:3).

The Holy Prophet s.a.w. assured them:

> If you will accept the message I have brought it will be for you a source of good luck in this world and in the Hereafter (Ibn Hisham, Vol. 1).

The Holy Prophet s.a.w. gave further substance to this concept of good luck on another occasion before his uncle, Abu Talib in this manner:

> " I exhort them (the Quraish) for one thing only. It is something by dint of which the whole Arabia will submit to them and all

the non-Arabs will pay homage to them" (*Masnad Ahmad, Vol.I*).

Allah hath promised such of you as believe and do good works that He will surely make them to succeed (the present rulers) in the earth even as He caused those who were before them to succeed (others) and that He will surely establish for them their religion which He hath approved for them (22:55).

Faint not, nor grieve, for you will overcome them if you are (indeed) believers (3:139).

As a result of the fulfilment of these conditions of faith and good deeds how abundantly these Divine promises were materialised is a fact fully known to the world. It is an established fact of history that Islam gave to the Muslims everything they could possibly need.

Relation Between the Observance of Religion and Prosperity

These illustrations are enough to convince us that Islam bestows on its followers material prosperity also. But we may still be curious to know how it comes about? When religion orients one towards the Afterlife and wants him to be indifferent to this world, how is it that he attains success in this world as well? How is it that he maintains a firm grasp of the religion but at the same time enjoys the good things of this life also? In order to find but an answer to this question and to understand the complexity of this problem we have to advert to the fundamentals of the religion.

Firstly, wealth, honour, power and similar things which are regarded as the corner-stones of the prosperity of this world are not despicable by themselves. In fact these are the bounties of Allah. The Qur'an has regarded them as such. The 5th surah of the Qur'an, *al-Ma'ida* (The Table Spread), is an example in point. While making mention of the people of Israel it describes the honour and power they enjoyed in their past as the bounties of Allah:

Remember Allah's favour unto you, how He placed among you

Prophets, and made you kings (5:20).

Similarly in the verse 112 of the *Surah an-Nahl* (The Bee), the comforts of life and abundance of provision have been described as favours of Allah:

A township that dwelt secure and well content, its provision coming to it in abundance from every side, but it disbelieved in Allah's favours (16:112).

In the Surah *"al-Jumu'ah* (the Congregation)"* as well as in other verses on many occasions, these things have been called the favours of Allah:

Then disperse in the land and seek of Allah's bounty (62:10).

Secondly, man has been created as a Caliph and vicegerent of Allah and this office enjoins that he should keep the management of this world in his own hands and run it in accordance with the injunctions and pleasure of his Master (as has been discussed at length in the previous chapters).

If these two fundamental conditions are kept in view the question is solved to the extent that honour, wealth and power are not at all the things the concern of which may be contrary to religion and belief. The reason for this is that things which are bounties and favours of Allah cannot be forbidden to the pious people. In fact the Divine verdict in respect of such things is:

Say: such good things on the Day of Resurrection, will be only for those who believe during the worldly life (7:32).

It means that in fact only such people deserve these things who are obedient to Allah. If they are really the people who deserve these things how could they be denied access to them? One who knows Allah runs from His chastisement and not from His favour.

This is how the worldly honour and wealth are the favours and bounties of Allah. Let us keep in view the purpose of man's creation and see what it warrants? Allah has appointed man as His vicegerent and wants that he should use his authority in accordance with His commands so that His wish is fulfilled in this world, as it is to be fulfilled in other worlds. As long as such men exist in this world who are alive to this duty, it will be at variance with the Divine justice and wisdom that they should be deprived of the power and authority of this world. To entrust this power and authority to such men will be illogical, who deny this obligation, do not accept this position of vicegerency and stake a claim of their own independence or accept the supremacy of someone other than Allah. It is a plain fact but in view of its importance it has been made still more evident by Allah:

And verily We have written in the Scripture, after the Reminder: My righteous slaves will inherit the earth (21:105).

On the other hand it will not suit the dutiful and obedient of Allah that they ignore the attainment of power without which they cannot carry out the duties of Caliphate. Something whereon depends the real objective of their life is, not only pleasing but compulsory. If all these facts are kept in view it will become evident that a Muslim does not seek the welfare of the After-life alone. He deserves and demands the prosperity of this world as well. It will be something natural for a Muslim if he does so. This is actually the reason why every true and sensible Muslim makes the following prayer to Allah:

Our Lord! Give unto us in the world that which is good and in the Hereafter that which is good (2:201).

This prayer is certainly granted if he establishes that he deserves it.

Now there remains only one aspect of the question which needs clarification. If a Muslim deserves and demands the welfare of the Afterlife as well as of this world, which he certainly does, why do the Holy Qur'an and the Tradition condemn such a demand so frequently? What would be, in that case, the meaning of contending that a Muslim is one who keeps his eyes fixed on the Hereafter and does not allow any worldly gain to have preference over the After-life.

Answer to the first question is that the world which is so condemned and the demand of which is so despised, is different from the world, the welfare of which a Muslim deserves and demands. Islam despises and forbids those things which make a man forgetful of Allah and negligent of his religious duties. The world condemned in he Qur'an and the Tradition signifies such a world. Things which do not make a man unmindful of Allah and do not make him neglectful of his religious duties, but rather help him in their fulfilment, are not at all condemnable, nor have they been forbidden by the religion. Instead they are approved of and demanded. The Qur'an does not condemn them but regards them "good of the world", "good life" and "reward of the world". When the word "welfare of the world" is used for the Muslim it signifies such things. It may be argued that "forgetfulness of Allah" and "negligence of the religious obligations" relate to the self of man and not to "worldly things. One thing which may cause one to forget Allah may not affect others in the same manner. Ordinary men lose their balance even with a small amount of wealth but a man like Umar bin 'Abdul Aziz does not, for a moment, become forgetful of Allah even while looking after the greatest empire of his times. Therefore any classifi-cation of things as such cannot be made. The fact is that things like wealth, honour, power are not intrinsically evil and need not be arbitrarily shunned. Actually it is one's own thinking and use of these things which render them harmful for him. Since Islam assumes that a Muslim does not misuse these things, as they are bestowed upon him by Allah, and utilises them in accordance with His pleasure and commands, these things do not constitute the kind of world which is condemned. Instead they make up the world which is good and sanctioned.

The answer to the second question is that to prefer the Afterlife to the temporal life does not mean the abandoning of worldly life.

What it actually means is that in the pursuit of material gains, and after their attainment, one should not become so oblivious of the religious injunctions as to harm the interests of the After-life. Now as far as the requirements of faith and interests of the After-life are concerned they are such that they restrict the desires of man, restrain him from following his whims and enjoin him to sacrifice his worldly interests for the betterment of his After-life. Most certainly they are not of the kind that would forbid the worldly things in all their forms and quantities. In some of the Traditions a Muslim has been likened to a horse tied to a peg with a rope of limited length. Obviously, the condition of such a horse is not similar to the horse whose legs are tied to the peg so tightly that it is unable to move. While the former has a limited freedom of movement and can graze the grass within its reach, the latter is completely deprived of such a freedom. This example makes it abundantly clear that although a Muslim is enjoined to prefer the After-life to this world, the way to worldly welfare has been to a reasonable extent, kept open for him. That is to say that while the welfare of the After-life is the prime object of his life, the way Islam prescribes for its attainment does not ignore the welfare of the temporal life but is deeply involved it. A careful examination of the verse of the *Surah Al-i-'Imran* of the Qur'an referred above, will clearly show that those who are true believers and do good deeds are rewarded handsomely not only in the After-life but in this world also. The fact that a man who is a worshipper of Allah and prefers the Hereafter to this world is given a reward in this life is proof enough that welfare of the world is included in the promised reward. This is how the preference of the Hereafter in itself results in the welfare of this world. It does not cut him off from the worldly welfare.

An Essential Condition for Material Prosperity

In the end it may be reminded that true belief and good conduct are not only essential for the welfare of the Hereafter, they are also equally important for temporal welfare. It means that the doors of the worldly blessings are thrown open to someone only when he or she fulfils the preconditions of true belief and good conduct. This connection hardly needs any proof. It has been made clear in the preceding paragraph that among past nations whoever was promised the welfare of the world was subject to the fulfilment of these preconditions. When the Muslims were given the good tiding of victory over the infidels it was qualified with the words:"If you are true believers". When they were given a promise that they will be given ruling power, this was made with the clarification that this promise is only for those who qualify for it by virtue of their true belief and good conduct.

Allah hath promised such of you as belief and do good works (24:55).

In short while it is a general promise of Allah that He bestows upon the believers the welfare of the temporal world. He also prescribes a general principle for it which enjoins that the reward is subject to true belief and good conduct. It means that, leaving aside the matter of welfare in the Hereafter, even the welfare of the worldly life cannot be attained without true belief and good conduct. Even the success in worldly life cannot be achieved without recourse to religion. This principle applies to the individual as well as to the nations without exception: Individuals in their own life can only get the good things of temporal life, such as peace of mind, honour, popularity and other material necessities, when at least in their own capacity they cherish love for Allah and show preference for the Hereafter as Muslims should indeed do. The Holy Prophet *s.a.w.* elaborated this fact when he said:

"One who converges his worries into one worry—a worry of the After-life—Allah is enough for the management of His world. And one whose mind is perplexed with innumerable worries— worries of the thought and affairs of the world—Allah does not care where he is killed". (*Ibn Majah*).

Another saying of the Prophet *s.a.w.* further clarifies this fact in the following words:

"One who makes the After-life his ultimate aim, Allah sets his affairs right and makes his heart generous and this world bows to him in obedience" (*Ibn Majah*)

On the same principle a nation would also get welfare of their collective life--freedom, wealth, honour, international prestige--when in its collective capacity it really behaves as Muslims. It means that on the one hand it should be formed of men of true belief and good conduct and on the other hand it should have that strong collective organisation without which no community can take shape and this has been so emphatically enjoined by Allah and His Prophet *s.a.w.*

It would not be correct to assume that this condition applies uniformly to all nations. Others can attain the highest degree of power in spite of all their transgressions but such a laxity on the part of Muslims is not excusable. For there is one and only one way for attaining power and it is through Islam. It is the way of submission to Allah. The straight path that leads to the witness of the truth. The reason for this difference is that Allah has not prescribed the same rule for the rise and decline of the Muslim people as He has done for the others. For others this rule is that if they cultivate amongst themselves some basic moral values and adopt means essential for the material progress they can rise to great heights but in the case of Muslims such things are not considered sufficient because Muslims are the flag-bearers of the religion of Allah and responsible for bearing witness to the Truth before the other nations. No other nation enjoys this position. This difference of position calls for a difference in rights and obligations. The difference in their rights and obligations naturally demands that the rules laid down for them should be different. If other nations deviate from the right path the justice demands that this offence of theirs is not considered as grave and serious a crime as it would be if committed by Muslims. It is, therefore, quite natural that while the other nations have been given the latitude that they can prosper even without obeying Allah the Muslims have been denied any such concessions. A nation endowed with the special bounty of Allah must also be subjected to the Divine wrath if it does not value the Divine Gift it is endowed with. The Qur'an has discussed at length this part of the Divine principles in respect of the Holy Prophet *s.a.w.* and his pious wives (may Allah be pleased with them all).

The fact that the Muslim nations can only attain power and glory in this world only when it really behaves as a nation submissive is borne out by the history of the last thirteen and a half centuries. As long as Muslims behaved as true Muslims they enjoyed such political power and economic affluence which even America and Russia do not enjoy today. As they declined from the position of "a nation submissive" to an ordinary nation, they lost their eminent position. So much so that they have now reacted a stage where they have become insignificant. This position is by itself indicative of the fact that the Muslims will not remain their true glory unless they transform themselves. The decision of Allah in respect of the people of the Scripture which He conveyed to them through the Holy Prophet *s.a.w.* is before us. He declares:

> *O People of Scripture! ye have not (of guidance) till Ye observe the Torah and the Gospel and that was revealed unto you from your Lord* (5:65).

This verdict is also indicative of the future of the Muslims and a nation. If they fail to re-establish the true religion by the Qur'an, the Divine law warrants that they would not be considered to be on the right path. Nor shall they be considered to be worthy of the respect and power for which Allah has promised to them as Muslims.

The future of the Muslims can only be different from their present if they go back to their past. They will be endowed with the gifts of true honour and power only if they let the religion of Allah dominate their lives. When the religion of their mosques is the same as is the religion of their parliament and assemblies. The Divine promise is always there to be fulfilled. Whenever the Muslims will earnestly desire and endeavour for it, it will be fulfilled.

It will be worthwhile to bear in mind another Divine law also. It enjoins that national freedom, respect and glory is bestowed upon a nation and not on individuals. This is the reason why Divine promise for these things has been made to the people and not to the individuals. If the Muslims are such a people as is required by Allah and His Prophet *s.a.w.*, that is to say, if they are true believers, righteous in their conduct and bear witness to the Truth they will certainly enjoy respect and freedom. They will be held in great esteem and wield great power. But if they are not such people they will not see the worldly blessings of Islam even if they be as innumerable as the atoms. Nor would the piety of a few of their individuals benefit them. The good and the bad and the active and the idle elements of the society shall equally share such a plight. It is possible that the pious and the active among them may go on getting the worldly blessings individually. Apart from the misdeeds committed by them in their collective capacity, and the evil conse-quences ensuing from them, the individuals must get the worldly blessings if they fulfil the prerequisites prescribed in this behalf. True that the pearls hidden beneath the mound of worthless stones will not transform the whole rough mass into a gilded crown but even in the midst of the mound the pearls will be able to retain their glitter and worth.

A Confusion and its Removal

What has been said in respect of the worldly prosperity can be viewed with scepticism and doubt by those who are in the habit of seeing things only superficially. They may contend that such a claim is not verified by experience. Numerous instances can be quoted of such persons who are good Muslims yet their life is very ordinary, and is even spent mostly in great hardships. As opposed to them, there are Muslims who have only a remote interest in Islam but are rich and enjoy great fame. Similarly some Muslim countries who do not bother to call themselves Muslim even for name's sake are independent and powerful whereas those Muslim countries wherein Islamic law is enforced are dependent on others. In such cases the promises and principles of prosperity and affluence are not intelligible. It will be pertinent to remove the confusion which arises in such cases.

As far as the welfare of the individuals is concerned it confuses only those who are unaware of the Islamic concept of "Material prosperity". This concept indeed greatly differs from the ordinary concept of prosperity. The right approach will be that in this respect we first acquaint ourselves with this concept. We find its detail in those verses of the Qur'an which carry the promise of prosperity for a true Muslim:

Whosoever doeth right, whether male or female, and is a believer, him verily We shall quicken with good life (16:197).

Whoso followeth My guidance, he will not go astray nor come to grief. But he who turneth away from remembrance of Me his will be a narrow life (20:122-123).

These verses disclose that the welfare of this world which a man gets by virtue of his faith and good conduct is "good life". It is a life free of tension and anxiety. In other words it does not lie in the abundance of material wealth, palatial houses, cavalcades of cars, armies of servants, rich food and costly dresses. Instead it comprises the necessities of life and contentment of heart. A wealth which makes one dependent on sleeping pills for sleep, which makes the mind a storehouse of worries and which keeps the heart ablaze with fear and greed cannot be regarded as such by any stretch of imagination. It is in fact the worst of agony. Such a wealth is not a source or prosperity but lands one in a miserable plight. One gets this kind of wealth when he abandons the love of Allah and stops striving for the betterment of his After-life. In consequence of his defalcation he gets a wealth whereby he becomes poorer than a starving creature and worse than a wretched soul. Against that, a man whose heart is full of love for Allah and which feels pleasure in striving for the betterment of the Afterlife, is as good as blessed with King Solomon's wealth even if he gets only a bare living. He is so blessed because the wealth which we call the peace of mind, emanates from the remembrance of Allah.

Verily in the remembrance of Allah do hearts find rest (13:28).

If one's heart is not negligent in the remembrance of Allah, he will certainly attain piety and one who is endowed with piety has a firm promise from Allah that he will not be wanting in food and clothes. Allah has assured that it is His responsibility to see that such a person is provided with his needs.

And whosoever keepeth his duty to Allah, Allah will appoint a way for him. And will provide for him (a quarter) whence he hath no expectation (65:2-3).

As far as the collective welfare of a society as a whole is concerned it is something so ordinary that it hardly deserves a mention. Such Muslim countries which show no love for Islam and claim to be independent and powerful are only wearing a mask of independence and power. In fact they are neither free nor powerful. While some of them are dependent on America, the others are supported by Russia. If this is the kind of independence and power they enjoy, Islam is sick of such a concept of freedom and power.

Similarly those Muslim states which are Governed by Islamic Law but appear to be weak and dependent on other powers are not Islamic States in the true sense. None of them can be truly regarded as an Islamic State. None of them has the courage to adopt Islamic laws in the vital social affairs of life. What we actually find is that they apply the Islamic laws to certain social and religious matters only. Obviously, such a partial application of Islamic laws is not a mark of certitude and firm faith. It is rather a sign of lack of confidence and incomplete faith. Allah has prescribed humiliation for such infirmity and has not extended any promise of power and glory to those who partially accept the Islamic system. If such Muslim countries happen to be the stooges of big powers they really deserve this position. Their half-hearted and partial enforcement of Islamic order will never yield real freedom and power to them. It is a reward which is endowed when Islamic system is fully adopted and enforced because the promise of Allah is subject to this condition. In respect of His promises He has exhorted the believers:

Fulfil your (part of the) covenant and I shall fulfil My (part of the) covenant (2:40).